DUCATI

DECIO GIULIO RICCARDO CARUGATI

DUCATI

DESIGN IN THE SIGN OF EMOTION

MONDADORI

Cover
Multistrada

Graphic Design
Dario Tagliabue

Page Layout
Elisa Seghezzi

Editorial Coordinator
Caterina Giavotto

Editing
Gail Swerling
Alessandra Raggio

Photograph Research
Lucia Impelluso

Technical Coordinator
Mario Farè

Quality Control
Giancarlo Berti

Translation
Richard Sadleir
Judith Spencer

Special thanks to
Vasco Premaor, Ducati Milano,
via Tertulliano 3
and to Irene Giorgi

www.mondadori.com/libri/

New expanded edition
© 2005 by Mondadori Electa S.p.A., Milan
Mondadori Libri Illustrati

In accepting the publisher's invitation to write this book, I have tried to bring out the artifice of Ducati as the supreme plaything, prompter of styles and forms of behavior. I found accomplices in all those lifelong adolescents—writers, poets, journalists, engineers, designers, musicians and artists—who have suffered and joyed, who have delighted and still delight and suffer for those magical red toys designed and built at Borgo Panigale. Many voices will be woven into my narrative without one drowning out the others, all uniting to consecrate the legendary sound of the Ducati engines. I wish to thank Marco Montemaggi and Giuliano Pedretti for their scrupulous reconstruction of the chronology of the key production models; Claudia Guenzani for acting as my precious contact inside the firm; and Livio Lodi for his helpfulness in securing me these contacts, indispensable in reconstructing the literature about the champions that I describe, and also for his patient compilation of the relevant illustrations. I have also tried to give expression to the emotions experienced by those who have written about Ducati's history, which runs from the Cucciolo of 1946 to the Monster, the 916, the MH900e, the Multistrada, the 999 and the Sportclassic, now entering the third millennium as outstanding embodiments of an evolutionary arc, their bloodlines still much in evidence. Of this evolution Carlotta Cavalieri Ducati, a biologist and the granddaughter of Bruno Ducati, the firm's founder with his brothers Adriano and Marcello, in far-off 1925, says: "It can be observed with the eyes of the great evolutionary scientists, who asserted that the forms of living creatures are the outcome not just of a process of invention but the gradual adaptation of previously existing forms."
I wish to thank Dario Tagliabue for his painstaking care of the book's graphics; Caterina Giavotto, Elisa Seghezzi, Gail Swerling, Alessandra Raggio, Lucia Impelluso, Giancarlo Berti and, in the person of Stefano Peccatori, the whole of Electa's editorial staff.

Decio Giulio Riccardo Carugati

Chronology of Key Models

1946 Cucciolo

1958 Elite 200

1961 Scrambler

1971 750 GT

1980 Pantah 500

1987 851

1993 Monster

1993 Supermono

1994 916

2000 MH900e

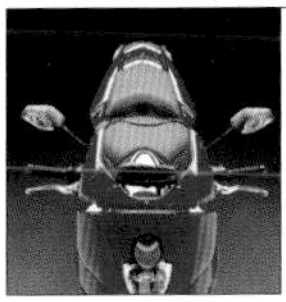

2001 Multistrada

2002 999

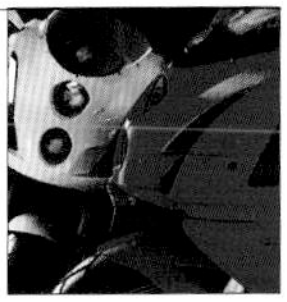

2003 Sportclassic

In *Impazienza*, the fine tale by Mario Colombi Guidotti (1922–1955), two youngsters are passengers aboard a clanking, ramshackle train, "in the bright, clear, early-morning sunshine" one day in July 1945, as it approaches Bologna station. "It crawled across a creaking, makeshift bridge spanning a dry ravine, gray with gravel and dusty sand, spotted with bushes and weeds. And then we saw the city, straight ahead of us, framed in the beautiful design of its hills. The stunned immobility of the countryside, the cracks at the bottoms of the bomb craters, the devastated walls of abandoned farmhouses were all forgotten, images that lay behind us. Now we encountered the spirited vitality of bare-chested workmen, toiling, smiling, making eloquent gestures with hands dirty with mortar. The city still preserved its clear colors, its severe bell towers, its soaring factory chimneys, and its ancient roofs, flashing like pieces of tin in the sun."

Miraculously unscathed by war, the city's ancient architecture emerges from the landscape of desolation. "The train slowly stretched out its length along an embankment, winding gently through a bare, parched hollow skirting the devastated outer city, while my gaze still probed the strangely compact and living body of the town. I snuffed up the scents of rusting iron, of brick and burnt wood, the smell of slow decay produced by the rain and sunshine, by the grass and the weeds, as we were pulling into what used to be the marshaling yards of the station. The skeletons of freight trucks, many still tied down, encumbered part of the shattered, twisted rails, while

The factory at Borgo Panigale before World War II: Ducati was founded for precision engineering and serial production.

the locomotives heaped up like beetles in a nest were blackening in their cemetery in a corner of the yards. In this place triumphed the most bizarre and irrational destruction and the most prostrate resignation of man. On a post, recently repainted, we saw a green signal framed in an eye, and we began our survey of all those unserviceable things."

To the north of the city the fury of war devastated the borough of Borgo Panigale. "October 12, 1944 was a clear, serene day," recalls Bruno Cavalieri Ducati in *Storia della Ducati*, his history of the Ducati firm. "At midday we heard a great noise and the sky grew black with Flying Fortresses. A few minutes later wave after wave of bombers unleashed enormous masses of high-explosive bombs on the Ducati factories. Within an hour everything was destroyed."

In that one hour this sudden, terrifying air raid had wiped out one of the most advanced Italian production facilities. Nine years earlier, in June 1935, on the land earmarked for the factory "the sickle had cut down the last stands of wheat," says Bruno, "and at once construction began. The design was modern and linear. At the front of the building, facing the Via Emilia, stood the Administrative Block. Behind it stretched a central corridor leading to the factory sheds where the various phases of production and assembly took place. On the left were the Staff Buildings, first of all the Technical School, then the locker rooms, canteens, kitchens and Social Services and First Aid Room, all fully equipped. There was even a dentist."

The Staff Buildings lined the road that was later

("It was an object of admiration / even including the organization. / The workers, to be frank, / had never donned white coats before, / but here this was the prescription / for doing work of precision.") The Ducati firm was thus founded on a philosophy of precision serial production.

named after Antonio Cavalieri Ducati, the father of Adriano, Bruno and Marcello.

"And so, after attending the School, receiving health care and changing into his work clothes, the Ducati worker would enter the factory. White, gleaming and spacious, it was very welcoming. On the walls of the long, broad corridors were illuminated signs that would raise a smile nowadays: Walk Fast, Speak Softly, No Smoking. In a serious, productive atmosphere, everything spoke of precision and diligent labor: there was no bending of the rules. On the right a private road ran parallel to Via Antonio Ducati: ranged along it for about 700 yards were the buildings for the preliminary or accessory phases of production: foundry, paintwork, carpentry, accessories and deliveries. The road ended in the big factory forecourt where goods were loaded and unloaded. Between Via Antonio Ducati and this private road, separated down the middle by the central passageway that started from the Head Office, there were machine shops for the different processes and products, each named after some great Italian: Galileo, Torricelli, Alessandro Volta, Luigi Galvani, Guglielmo Marconi, Cardano. Twenty factory sheds in all, each with its specialty. There would be a Department Foreman and a Production Program for each Ducati product. There was also a Measurement Center, a special air-conditioned room with the most modern instruments all calibrated to the thousandth of a millimeter."

Dino Berti wrote a celebratory jingle in the dialect of Bologna, vaunting the factory's achievements. Bruno quotes it in his *Storia della Ducati*. "…Al fo' ugèt d'amiraziàn/ anch par l'urganizaziàn:/ l'operèri, a èser franch,/ in avéven mai fsté 'd bianch,/ mo qué l'éra ed prescriziàn / lavurand ed prezisiàn." /

In 1925, the brothers Cavalieri Ducati—with less than fifty years among the three of them—and their partner Carlo Crespi founded the Società Scientifica Radio. Its aim was to provide a field for the inspired research of Adriano, the eldest, then a young physics student, and to manufacture the Manens condensers of his invention.

"Antonio Cavalieri Ducati," Bruno explains, "was an engineer who took a keen interest in his sons' industrial venture. He had inherited some property in Florence from his brother Gaetano. This he sold and used the capital to give an appropriately modern framework to their budding radio-electrical factory. With a few friends he formed a regular joint-stock company and in 1926, amid the stir created by Guglielmo Marconi's return to Bologna to receive an honorary degree from the university, the company papers were signed before the *notaio* Marani. It now became the Società Scientifica Radio Brevetti Ducati for the development of patents granted to Adriano Cavalieri Ducati. The capital was subscribed by the *Onorevole Cavaliere avvocato* Attilio Loero, *Conte ingegnere* Adolfo Aria Branca, *Grande Ufficiale avvocato* Attilio Scotti, *ragioniere* Renzo Ficcarelli, *Grand Ufficiale dottore* Roberto Villetti, *Commendatore dottore* Tito Francia

Cucciolo

Comi, *Cavaliere* Temistocle Tito Pasquini, *Grande Ufficiale dottore* Lodovico Bertani."

Adriano had given early proof of his talent: when just twenty years old he established the first bilateral short-wave link between Italy and the United States. The Italian Admiralty took a close interest in his research, which enabled a ship on the high seas to keep in touch simultaneously with five continents.

"In October 1926," recalls Bruno, "the Ducati firm rented three ground-floor rooms on Via Collegio di Spagna 9 in Bologna. You came off the street into a courtyard at the center of the premises. Access was by a glass door with a bell fixed to the top that rang when someone came in. Inside there was a counter of normal height above which barely emerged the face of a little secretary. She was called Bice Tartarini and dressed like a schoolgirl, in a black smock and white collar. From the entrance you passed into two big rooms, one on the right, the other on the left. The first was where I worked together with Adriano and—when he got back from his delivery round—Marcello. We two would sign the letters underneath the seal, like big firms or banks, one on the right and the other on the left. One day the bell rang and in the doorway appeared an elegant gentleman wearing a big sombrero and carrying a rich, ivory-handled walking stick. 'El Señor Ducati?' he asked. He was an Argentine, straight from Buenos Aires, on his way to Bergamo to visit the graves of his ancestors. He had decided to stop off in Bologna and give in an order for some Manens condensers, of which he had received a sample. Bice rushed to call us and we ushered him into our office. He said he had met Adriano in Buenos Aires: first during the visit of an Italian ship which held the record

1940, Raselet.
The first electric razor made in Italy.

for being the first to transmit from the ocean to the five continents and then at a lecture on short waves he delivered at the Academy of Sciences in Buenos Aires. Our visitor's name was Mario Argento and he owned the biggest emporium for the sales of radio parts in Argentina. He had gotten his technicians to test the Manens condenser and kept saying, '*Muy bonito, muy bonito*. Send me three thousand pieces. I'll get my bank in Buenos Aires to send you a letter of credit.' Adriano and I were staggered, but also a bit worried, because if he had asked, as was natural given the size of

1942, film projector.
"High-precision items revealing the rare and consummate skill of workers and technicians, a school of engineering founded and developed."
Marco Montemaggi

16

the order, to inspect our 'factory,' we would certainly have been in trouble. At that time it was in the cellar of our house on Viale Guidotti. Nothing of the kind, however. He took his leave ceremoniously and went on his way in the same courtly fashion as he had arrived."

The factory, far from existing when Mario Argento lodged his order, soon took shape. It had floor space of two hundred square meters and employed over a hundred workmen. The Manens fixed condensers were soon joined by variable condensers which called for the working of aluminum alloy for the production of the plates and their construction. Later, when production moved to the new facility at Borgo Panigale, the Ducati brothers purchased a Genèvoise spot welder and punch which did away with the need to grind and buff the constituent parts of the condensers. This was the birth of that precision engineering that was to give luster to the Ducati firm. Who better than Dino Berti, in his popular rhymes, to celebrate the history of a firm that at the war's end provided jobs for so many people under the shadow of Bologna's twin towers? "La Ducati l'as fé unour/ con un nóv condensadour/ ban, putant, banché cinén/ 'd la grandazza ed du suldén./ Se int la radio

as éra usè/ un'antanna cunplichè/ fata ed stangh e balanzén/ soul un'asta e un brazadlén/ la fé vadder ch'léra asè/ pr'aguantèr l'anda zarchè./ An dscuràn di muturén/ ch'l'ai n'à fat di grand di cén/ e po dl'ótica spezièl/ sàmper nóva, uriginèl./ Al prudótt, a inción secand,/ l'é stimè par tótt al mand./ La Ducati, con passiàn, sampr'in zairca ed perfeziàn, la và drétt par la so strè: póst ch'l'unoura la zitè/ ai dan dis int la pagèla,/ tóch e dai la zirudèla." ("At Ducati they made a splash / with a new condenser / good and powerful, though tiny / no bigger than a coin. / If a radio used a complicated aerial/ made of a staff and a cross-arm, / now just a rod and circlet / as they showed was enough / to find the wave you sought. / We won't mention all the motors / which they've made, big and small, / and then the special optical instruments, / always new and original. / The product, second to none, / is esteemed in all the world. / Ducati, with passion / always in search of perfection / goes straight ahead on its way. / Since it honors the city, / give it ten out of ten / and sing its praises.")

The train that pulled into Bologna station, so powerfully evoked by Mario Colombi Guidotti, ran along rails that seemed to lead through devastation and over great gaping

In the 1940s: display of Ducati products at the Izmit Enternasyonal Fuari, Istanbul.

chasms. This was the same spectacle that appeared to the Ducati brothers when, in May 1945, they returned to Bologna from evacuation in Boarezzo in the province of Varese.

"When I agreed to attempt to reconstruct the memory of Ducati," declares Marco Montemaggi, "and describe the firm's development of designs and products from the war's end up to the present, I said that certainly I would have to record how Adriano, Bruno and Marcello decided to rebuild the firm, resolving not to surrender to the desolating spectacle of the factory reduced to rubble, and how, once the war was over, in a short time and despite their personal troubles they recreated the conditions for the company's development. But even before this they had struggled in wartime to prevent the factory-workers from being deported to Germany together with the plant."

Bruno himself told the writer of those decisive moments. "The workers' occupation of the factory at Borgo Panigale, on September 9, 1943, was followed by the order of the German High Command to dismantle the plant and transfer it to Germany. On September 27 the Reich's Plenipotentiary for Radio Communications sent us a dispatch which named the localities where our requisitioned factories would be sent to in Germany and Austria. It was only thanks to two of our executives who spoke excellent German, Dr. Legeza and Dr. Leardini, that we managed to persuade the High Command of the difficulties involved in this sudden decentralization of production. We were playing for time, preventing the deportation of the workers and the transfer of irreplaceable equipment which would be irrecoverable at the war's end and essential if we were to restart production. So we played along and faked compliance with the objective of relocating to Germany by moving most of the plant to our factory at Parona Valpolicella, in the province of Verona, as if it was on its way to their final, compulsory destination. In actual fact, from Parona the equipment was sent to Cavalese in Trentino, Longare near Vicenza, and Pianezza in Turin. In only a few months we had evacuated the factories at Borgo Panigale, Crespellano and Bazzano, and the staff and equipment were safely in secret warehouses, over seventy of them underground. Not one worker was deported, not one of our precious machines was lost. The bombing raids found the factories empty."

The CNLAI (Committee for the Liberation of Northern Italy, a partisan body) and the Allies misunderstood the real aims of the Ducati brothers. This created a very difficult situation for the firm. Even complete acquittal on charges of collaborating with the enemy failed to entirely dispel suspicion.

In *Ducati, una Moto un Mito un Museo*, Marco Masetti takes up the story after the war. "By committing themselves heavily, especially in financial terms, and sacrificing a large part of the family's estate, the Ducati brothers managed to regain control of the firm. As early as 1946 at Borgo Panigale they had started producing the first Cucciolo clip-on engines for bicycles … The work force rose close to its prewar figure with a total of over 4500 employees."

All this was achieved without state contributions to compensate for wartime damage suffered by the firm, assessed at about 500 million liras in the values of the period.

"The firm had already passed many milestones in the two decades before construction of the factory for producing the Cucciolo engine. The two condensers, fixed and variable," as explained by Marco Montemaggi, "were joined in 1932 by an electrolytic condenser and, in 1935, the Manens reservoir. In 1930 it began production of the Radiostilo, a unified

1946, Cucciolo auxiliary engine.
The Cucciolo with its compact and effective design, was applied to the bicycle, the commonest means of transport at the time, with its reliable setup.

anti-static antenna, and in 1935 the Dufono, an intercom which solved the problem of communications in offices and did away with the need for employees to telephone each other. In 1939 the firm began production of the Ducati Musical Radio Set and in 1940 the Raselet, the first electric razor made in Italy, to an American license. In 1941 it launched the Ducati Microcamera; in 1942 it started production of the Duconta, a very advanced calculating machine, and the Ducati Film Projector. These were high-precision items that revealed the rare and consummate skill of the workers and technicians, a school of engineering founded and developed. After the war, the firm's distinctive culture undoubtedly gave the Cucciolo factory an edge over its competitors."

It was the example of the Cucciolo, born out of an exclusive tradition of precision engineering, that developed Ducati's awareness of engines and eventually led it into motorcycle design proper.

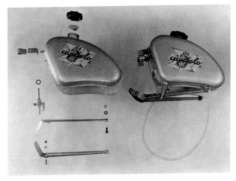

Exploded view and fuel tank with the bracket of the Cucciolo auxiliary engine.

"The drought of 1947," continues Masetti, "caused cuts in hydro-electricity supplies which interrupted production. Then the firm was heavily in debt to the banks, which forced the Cavalieri Ducati family to call for an increase in the company's capital and at last turn to the FIM (the government's Engineering Industry Fund). The Fund agreed to a rescue package provided the firm went into receivership. The Ducati brothers were offered honorary posts but little else. Adriano and Marcello were made General Consultants while Bruno became Managing Director, in this case a purely symbolic post. Despite steady growth in the motorcycle sector, the Fund's administration and labor troubles on the shop floor led in the short space of one year to bankruptcy proceedings."

Bruno writes the words that sounded the knell of the company. "What happened next baffles the understanding. That Bologna was in the sights of secret agents as the starting

point for a vast subversive operation is possible but there is no proof of it. There may have been a plot afoot to cripple Ducati and Bolognese industry but there is no evidence that this was so. It remains an enigma."

He rehearses the facts, which certainly fail to shed light on the mystery. The chapter is titled "Chronology of a Spoliation": "February 28, 1949: Mantelli, the Receiver, orders the closure of the Ducati plants. This causes an immense stir. The reasons behind the shutdown are far from clear. The President of the FIM insists there will be no further credit lines unless several hundred workers are first fired. The unions, the firm's executives, and the workers protest that the growing demand for Ducati products means that working hours ought logically to be increased. Patrignani had drawn up the firm's development plan in agreement with the Ducati brothers: he resigns rather than be the accomplice of a Receiver who wants to sack workers. March 8, 1949 is the first anniversary of the institution of the receivership. Given the way the Receiver had fixed matters there was only one solution, to apply for bankruptcy. The President of the FIM comes to an agreement with the Compagnia Finanziaria di Partecipazione, which holds advances on long-term financing from the FIM, and drafts an application for a composition with creditors at the expiry of the receivership. After this there will be all the time to complete the takeover of the shares in the Ducati company. March 15, 1949: the Milan Bankruptcy Court, Judge Consoli presiding, admits the Ducati company to the benefit of a composition with its creditors after the FIM deposits 750 million lire with the banks and Dr. Nello Gerosa of Milan is appointed administrator by the court. The Ducati brothers—who have given their guarantee to the banks—were left to their mercy. Giovanni Gallarati, of the Compagnia Finanziaria di Partecipazione, in his role as the new Managing Director named by the

Board of Directors goes to the prefect of Bologna to report on the immediate reopening of the Ducati factories and the payment of arrears of wages to all the firm's employees. December 1949: the Compagnia Finanziaria di Partecipazione sells the FIM all the shares it holds as collateral for the financing."

Marco Masetti winds up the story: "The Ducati family, by this time ousted from the running of the firm, submits to its expropriation by the Italian state and seeks new paths. Adriano leaves for the United States, where he conducts research into electronics in the aerospace sector. Marcello remains in the field of electrical engineering; Bruno continues to work as an engineer in the fields of nuclear energy, safety, advanced studies, research and patents."

When I called on Bruno in his Milan home, he received me with great courtesy and confided, without a shadow of complacency or boastfulness: "I am close on a hundred years old. I want to ask the Mayor of Bologna to receive me in the palace of King Enzo, in what used be my father Antonio's study. A predecessor had presented it to him for his merits. Together with the whole of Ducati we will celebrate my hundredth birthday." His lips and eyes are smiling, but a shadow of sadness traverses them. "Adriano and Marcello are no longer there, they are already part of the fable. I'm the only one left, the only witness to Ducati's history." Bruno puts on his spectacles and in a firm voice reads the Afterword to his history: "When—many years ago—I was asked to write this history, I smiled and said: 'No, no, let's not talk about all that. It's a fable.' Then I added: 'And once written it won't be a fable any more.' Now that I have finished writing it I wonder if this is really History or if it remains a fable. There must be a grain of truth in this misgiving, since—even quite recently—other historians have been

called on to write the more hermetic pages that I have omitted. I am myself happy and curious about it: after suffering so much I still have not got my own back on all those who fail to share my enthusiasm for my city, for its industriousness and genius. I have not yet succeeded in explaining why Rolandino de' Passeggeri, who revived Roman Law at the University of Bologna, Luigi Galvani, who discovered electricity in Bologna, or Guglielmo Marconi, who began here in Bologna the great electronic era which has changed the world, should be signs of the distinctive intelligence of the Bolognesi, made to be guides to other men. And this brings us, modestly, to precision engineering, the first among many products. With this hymn of faith I desire not to arrest the fable, in the hope that it will always be cultivated and honored."

So the Ducati brothers were swept away, in the immediate postwar period, by paradoxical events wholly alien to their invincible desire for the good of the firm. But the skills they had built up, that legacy of achievements with their roots in Adriano's technical school, were not dispelled by these events. The heritage was not frittered away by the incoming executives, though they were quite unaware of its inestimable value. The work-

"If you want to come with me / I'll take you on my Cucciolo / the motorcyle's tiny / but it throbs just like my heart."

Pioneer among the pioneers:
Mario Recchia, race rider
and mechanic at Ducati.

Circuito di Bari
9 . 5 . 1947
Recchia in piena velocità

ers and technicians were its jealous guardians. Out of their skills there grew the new developments at the Ducati precision engineering company.

As Melissa Holbrook Pierson writes in *The Perfect Vehicle*: "In this century, automobiles have done more to alter human society, culture and economy—not to mention the earth's landscape and even weather—than any single invention … Motorcycles have changed little of the world. But they require a different scale by which to measure their charge, a more personal one that registers on the ground of immediate experience. At some times and in some places, the uses to which they were put were pragmatic and little else. But for much of their existence, and everywhere the automobile was prevalent, they have owed their presence to the active intervention of their proponents. At times, very active indeed."

Even more than the motorcycle, the bicycle is suited to practical humdrum uses. And for these purposes, the rider was spared the toil of providing its motive power by applying an engine to the bicycle, as an aid to and substitute for mere pedal power. The result was a kind of hybrid, which could be driven by either human or mechanical power. As for speed, it was no advantage in either case: the maximum

and minimum speeds corresponded to the measure of human strength. This is implicit in its name: "auxiliary," applied to a bicycle engine, renders fully the sense of this composite, eclectic form of transport. The engine-driven bicycle remained structurally within limits that did not allow it to bear stresses any greater than its rider could subject it to.

In his *Introduzione al design italiano* Andrea Branzi notes: "Italy has made a wholly original contribution to innovation in short-range types of transport, an industrial sector that was historically very rigid and little open to experiment … In Italy the classical cycle of technological research was reversed: during the war the British and American armies had already equipped their parachutists with folding mopeds, but in Italy the army had blocked prewar research by FIAT into the same products. These new engines, like starting motors for airplane undercarriages, tanks and the whole range of micro-engines misused in wartime, were retrieved after the war by a widespread network of inventors, designers and small entrepreneurs, who produced the Vespa, Lambretta and Cucciolo, the Oxis Prina and the Isetta bubble car. They had in mind a market for mass mobility that was developing in heterodox terms: the designers were look-

The Cucciolo triumphs
in New York, 1947.

ing for a short cut through the established types of products and inventing forms of evolutionary behavior outside the tradition. They revealed a flair for grasping real opportunities in an abstract, invented, potential scenario: and though this was not yet actual, it proved capable of nurturing the novelty represented by the product."

In *Vola Colomba*, Gian Franco Venè (1935–1992) writes: "Every evening, before the time signal, the radio transmitted a jingle for two voices which girls used to sing while washing the dishes: 'Se vuoi venir con me/ ti porterò sul Cucciolo/ il motorino è piccolo/ ma batte come il mio cuor'. ('If you want to come with me / I'll take you on my Cucciolo / the motorcycle's tiny / but it throbs just like my heart.') In

Though the Cucciolo came in a do-it-yourself kit, mounting it was a job for a mechanic, who also guaranteed the reliability of this composite means of transport. And it was applied to the commonest vehicle of the day, the bicycle, whose tried and tested setup required no modification.

"For 39,000 lire (at 1946 values) you got a 48cc four-stroke engine; but potential buyers were unconcerned about these technical specifications: the essential thing for those who contented themselves with a Cucciolo was that they could get around on a bike even if they were old and their knees had seized up because of rheumatism."

This covered one group of customers, who were certainly not tempted by a desire for thrills and speed. The Cucciolo

Linked to the pedals of the common bicycle, the Cucciolo enhanced its scope and symbolized an improved quality of life.

those days language was grayer but more precise: to modern Italians a 'motorino' means a scooter or motorcycle, but originally it meant a small auxiliary engine. So when they imagined the Cucciolo, no one bothered about what it looked like: it was sold in a box, together with a sort of can that served as the fuel tank and a big pedal with the drive gear that meshed with the inside of the wheel. It could be fitted to any bicycle and only a mechanic could do it."

"didn't putter, it hummed along: on a flat asphalted road it could do almost 40 kph and it could do 70 kilometers with a liter of gasoline costing a hundred lire. It could take the weight of a second person sitting on the cross bar or the carrier; but when going uphill the passenger had to get off and the rider had to help it with the pedals. It boasted two gears. To change up or down you had to kick back on the pedal and once you developed the knack you could do it

without inflicting any damage." Gian Franco Venè studies, distinguishes and compares, seeking to identify the different uses of the bicycle and the motor-bicycle after World War II. He identifies the groups of aficionados of each of these forms of transport. "An extremely old-fashioned kind of advertisement, modest and confined to the popular papers, urged unskilled workers to get ahead by enrolling in a correspondence school for electricians. It depicted a man straddling a motorbike with a sidecar. 'I had no prospect of a career and my pay was low,' says the blurb. 'Is it worth going on like this? I wondered. I enrolled in the School and now, thanks to the diploma, I do a clean job, my neighbors respect me and I can afford to own this motorbike.' In reality a sort of social prejudice weighed on the motorcycle. In the past nearly everyone's image of a motorbike was of a rough, dirty, dangerous vehicle with a big engine that made a terrific racket and was quite rudimentary, absolutely uncomfortable, and hence suited to people accustomed to labor who could afford to turn up at work with dirty, oily hands and poorly dressed. Like cars, postwar motorbikes hadn't changed much; or if they had, only mechanics and a few motorbike buffs noticed the difference. Motorcycles used for the honest purpose of getting to work were rarely new and shiny. They had two seats aligned, the back one raised higher, and mudflaps; these were two wobbly metal aprons at the sides of the forks which showed their owner's indifference to esthetics and speed. There was nothing much about these vehicles to tempt a youngster; they were the final prize of workmen promoted to shop foremen, of tradesmen, farm managers, butchers, middle-aged people who wore over their patched and mended jerseys a scuffed leather coat of a kind never seen since the days of chauffeurs and horseless carriages."

Nor was it likely, "despite the jingle of the advertisement, that the Cucciolo would ever be used for elopements. It held out

DUCATI M55

MOTORE : a 4 tempi con valvole in testa.
Cilindrata : 48 cm.³
Rapporto di compressione : 6.7
Potenza : 1.35 C₂ a 5150 giri.
Accensione : a volano magnete con bobina per fanale e clacson.
Cambio : a due velocità a preselezione del folle con comando a richiesta.

Trasmissione : a catena unica utilizzante la stessa catena del ciclo sia per la trasmissione a motore sia per quella a pedale.
Lubrificazione : ad ingranaggio pescatore con serbatoio nel carter di 0.5 lt. di capacità.
Consumo : 1 lt. di benzina normale per 90 Km.
Velocità massima : 50 Km/h.

a manopola   a mano   a pedali

DUCATI MECCANICA S. p. A.   BOLOGNA - BORGO PANIGALE

no thrills to youngsters or even ensure clerks they could get to the office without smudging their trousers. In some way it enlarged the stigma already attached to motorbikes. On country roads you would meet with motor-bicycles overloaded with baskets of vegetables or brushwood. They were mostly used by middle-aged workmen. A lot of women, too, even elderly ones, with a scarf knotted under their chin and peasant shoes, used a Cucciolo to get about. It seems that thanks to the Cucciolo, half a million Italians between 1946 and 1950 learned to use an engine-driven vehicle."

So, curiously enough, the motorcycle and the motor-bicycle, though substantially different machines, managed to extend the traditional range of users through their everyday use, but they failed to change behavior in society at large.

Hence, "What was later to be clumsily and rather hastily described in the nineteen-fifties as the 'motorization of Italy' was not so much a sign of the spread of affluence as an earthquake in individual choices. A few years later the passengers on the Settebello Express would be surprised to see flashing by the windows the barren hedges of TV aerials erected on the roofs of shacks and see the disquieting opalescent glimmer of TV screens in hovels inhabited by families who barely knew what a radio set was ... They forgot that everything had begun when they themselves had first bought a motor scooter, skipping the compulsory stage of buying a bicycle and the optional stage of a Cucciolo or Mosquito."

The Mosquito in the period was the Cucciolo's direct competitor: "It consumed twice as much and used a more expensive fuel mixture," notes Venè. "It was also 10cc smaller. It permitted itself the luxury of working by a roller applied directly to the rear tire, wearing it out. It was even smaller than the Cucciolo. 'It could be used as an egg-beater,' someone said."

Of the two kits, the Cucciolo was more reliable both for durability and fuel-economy.

"No more roller rubbing against the tire, not even for the dynamo," shrilled an ad in *Motoclismo*. The blurb below the title said: "Cucciolo, the miraculous 4-stroke micro-engine, with overhead valves and automatic gear shift, the world champion for fuel economy. Now ready for delivery for the winter season with a new built-in dynamo for headlight and rear light at no extra charge."

The same magazine reviewed the bicycle engines presented at the Twenty-Fourth Bicycle and Motorcycle Show in 1946. "The Cucciolo, designed by the SIATA and mass-produced in collaboration with Ducati in Bologna, needs no further introduction. It is practically the only 4-stroke engine on the market and one of the commonest micro-engines. This shows a wide clientele now appreciates its merits: its refine-

Motociclismo published a letter from a Catholic priest in Udine which highlighted the Cucciolo's reliability. "I was filled with enthusiasm, above all after a long and varied tour with it from August 19 to 29 of this year. I covered about 1200 km in just six days of actual traveling, since the other days were stopovers. Starting from Udine and going via Carnia, the Canal di Gorto, Cima Sappada (1292 meters high) and the Pass of Monte Croce Comelico (1636 meters), I descended to Val Pusteria with a visit to the Lake of Braies (rising in 11 km from 1100 meters to 1495 meters with a 20% gradient, then went through Bressanone, Bolzano, Merano and the Val Venosta. I climbed up the Stelvio (2759 meters), where the engine displayed all its brio and power by coping brilliantly with the formidable ascent. In fact the Cucciolo sometimes got to places where not even the most powerful car could arrive: from the Hotel at Sotto Stelvio

ment and completeness, clean working, low fuel- and oil-consumption, the presence of a two-speed clutch gear-shift with semi-automatic control and pre-selector, smooth running, the regularity of the engine, and built-in dynamo for the lights. It should also be noted that the cheap cost of a machine is a function not so much of the greater or lesser complexity of the design as of the organization and potential of the means of production: everyone knows that in this respect the Ducati company has an immense potential." The article emphasizes the distinctive feature of Ducati products, the high degree of standardized production achieved by designing them for precision engineering. Ducati's company culture was remarkable when compared with the standards of the period.

At Ducati, the Cucciolo evolved into the motor which shed its pedals and became a moped.

the road was covered in snow and interrupted by about twenty different avalanches, obstacles that the lightness and handiness of the Cucciolo unit easily enabled me to overcome. The upshot was that I made tracks across the virgin snow well before anyone else. Quite alone I reached the summit (August 23, 4 p.m.) amid the admiration of many who had made the ascent on the other side, which had been cleared by the snowplow. So great was the enthusiasm that some of the others wanted to pose for a photo beside my gallant Cucciolo. Then came a vertiginous descent into Valtellina, followed by a tour of the Lakes of Como, Iseo and Garda, including excursions to Bergamo and Brescia, and on to Trent, the Valsugana, Belluno, Pieve di Cadore, and Passo

Mauria (1293). I returned fresh to Udine after doing 250 km on the last day. A checkered trip and not devoid of difficulties, yet I never had any trouble with the engine, which always responded well and coped easily. It was also economical. When I returned to Udine there was still a little of the thirteenth liter of fuel in the tank. This means I got an average fuel consumption of a liter for every 100 km. So I can only say I'm highly satisfied with the Cucciolo, which enabled me to have a magnificent holiday with a very moderate outlay. Yours sincerely, Father Giuseppe Scarbola."

After the Cucciolo, the climber of mountains, received this warranty from Father Scarbola of Udine, its triumph across the Atlantic in 1947 was certified in the travel notes of an engineer, Aldo Loria, quoted by Bruno in *Storia della Ducati*: "The day I left for New York I thought the old saying about taking coals to Newcastle could be given a

gled happily to answer. I now felt like a big player and thought: you're a real Cucciolo [the word means 'cub' in Italian] with the strength of a lion cub. And this is how the Cucciolo made its entry to New York."

Ah, the strength of the small! The Ducati micro-engine, just 48cc of cylinder capacity, could boast maximum reliability on long, winding roads. The "Cucciolo power unit," as Father Scarbola of Udine called it, could climb up rugged mountainsides and then handle the steep descent without any sign of strain. On the other hand, in those same years, one of the most celebrated and fêted motorbikes was a Norton 500 dubbed "La Poderosa II." The bike belonged to Alberto Granado who, with his friend Ernesto Che Guevara (1928–1967), set out on a north-bound journey along the roads and dirt tracks of the immense South American continent. Che kept a diary of the adventure: his descriptions of

modern twist as 'taking Cucciolo engines to New York.' I reflected rather sadly that there was little to envy in the lot of a man detailed off to sell engines in the land of engines. But I was wrong. I got the first inkling of my happy error the day I went through customs. Those fine customs officers had a rather patronizing air as they examined my belongings and the various samples I carried in my luggage. But then there was a sudden change of scene: from a heap of my personal effects emerged the Cucciolo. Instantly the four unbending customs officers forgot all about import duties, export prices and sworn declarations, and they started to inspect my engine with the fond gaze of a woman eyeing a cute little baby. They uttered exclamations and peppered me with questions which I strug-

the mishaps caused by the bike's many breakdowns reveal a definite comic flair. Here is a sample of the diary: "The motorbike struggled along, showing the strain inflicted on it, especially in the bodywork, where there was always something to be fixed using Alberto's favorite spare part, a piece of wire. I don't know where he picked up a saying he had fathered on Oscar Galvez: 'Wherever a bit of wire can be used instead of a screw I prefer it. It's more reliable.' Our trousers and hands showed by unmistakable signs that we shared Galvez's predilection for bits of wire. Night was falling and we hoped to find a village soon. The light was poor and sleeping rough was not a pleasant prospect. We were going slowly by the beam of the headlight when all at once we heard a strange noise we couldn't identify. The headlight was not enough to see what was making the noise. We guessed it must be a broken spoke. Stranded, we prepared to rough it for the night. We put up our tent and crawled inside, trying to forget we were hungry and thirsty (there was no water in the neighborhood and we had no food with us). Unfortunately the breeze freshened in the night and grew into a gale: it blew our tent over and left us at the mercy of the weather with the chill growing. We tied the motorbike to a telegraph pole and bedded down behind it, sheltering under the ground sheet. The gale even prevented the use of our camp beds. The night was far from pleasant but in the end exhaustion overcame even the cold, wind and everything else and we woke at nine the next morning with the sun already high. By daylight we could see that the dreadful noise had been caused by a gash in the frame at the front of the machine. The problem was how to patch it up and reach the nearest village where we could get someone to mend the broken tubing. Our friend, a bit of wire, helped us out of the fix for the time being. We collected all our things and set off without any idea of how far the nearest village might be. To our immense surprise, after the second bend we came to a house that was inhabited. They gave us a big welcome and we fleshed our teeth in a delicious joint of roast lamb. From there we did another twenty kilometers to a place called Piedra de Aguila where we found a welder."

The Cucciolo was definitely the most popular of all auxiliary engines in its day, as claimed in the refrain of the song by the Maestro Olivero. It was linked to the pedals of the bicycle, the commonest form of personal transport at that time, and made the bike far more useful for everyday purposes. So at least initially it was a highly useful and liberating invention—rather like the outboard engine which did away with the labor of rowing.

As the magazine pointed out at the end of its review of the Twenty-Fourth Cycle and Motorbike Show, the Cucciolo "is an engine that can be mounted either on an ordinary bicycle or on a special bicycle to create a sort of light motorcycle. The engine can also be supplied on request with a hub

with two gears spaced to give the cyclist a four-speed gear-shift. This makes for easy traveling in hilly and mountainous areas."

In the same issue Carlo Gabardi Brocchi noted: "The bicycle can be turned into a light motorcycle with pedals and full elastic suspension—something not even the French *velomoteur* or German *motorfahrrad* can boast, though they are widely used in those countries. This takes you into a completely different field which has nothing to do with an auxiliary engine yet costs little more than the good bicycle it ought to be mounted on. The increase in the power of some 'micro-engines' is clearly a sign of the times. In fact a micro-engine mounted on a sturdy bicycle, with thick tires and elastic suspension, can give can give much broader performance than an ordinary motorized bicycle and at the same time will always cost far less than a real light motorcycle."

So now the hybrid motor-bicycle was flanked by a vehicle that was no longer composite but specially designed for the engine. It was called a moped because of the pedals, used by the rider to start it up and rest his feet on when traveling. This was the beginning of the quest for a new potential for the micro-engine. It aroused misgivings, objections and protests, even among the experts, engineers such as Giuseppe Remondini, who had shown his knowledge of auxiliary motors in the early 1940s. *Motociclismo* published a letter from him on December 19, 1946. "As for the criteria and orientations of motorcycles in Italian industry, I have noted its developments with interest but have to conclude by quoting the technical expert of the French newspaper *L'Equipe*: when describing the micro-engines

The 1950s graphics add a stylish touch to the design of these Ducati mopeds.

col **65 DUCATI**
la crisi del petrolio
non interessa:

65 Km. con 1 lt. di benzina!

motoleggere DUCATI BOLOGNA

Suez

applied to bicycles at the Paris Motor Show he ended by commenting 'qu'on ne fait pas mal de bêtises.' In fact the problem is not to seek, by various shifts, to turn a bicycle into a motorbike but—as a rigorous presupposition—to preserve the bicycle's basic features of simplicity and lightness: tried and tested now for forty or fifty years. What is now needed is to simply replace the effort exerted by the cyclist with the force provided by a small engine which, however, should not in practice exceed the speed, power and performance originally supplied by the cyclist. If you increase the power of the engine, from a craze for speed or the desire to over-take your competitor (the people who have permitted or encouraged micro-engine races are plumbing the depths of stupidity), then it is no wonder you are immediately forced to add elastic front or back forks, a sprung seat, reinforced frame and so forth."

Remondini concluded by declaring he was confident of an imminent return to the original, auxiliary function of the micro-engine, suited to the scale of a bicycle. This was not to be, because the micro-engine eventually developed into the moped, with a clearly-defined configuration, and as such it has long been popular on the market for two-wheel-ers. While some firms specialized in mopeds in those years,

at Ducati the motor-bicycle was a transitional stage of design and production that developed through the light motorcycle, a step forward, into the motorcycle proper. What better describes the Ducati's evolutionary process than Francisco Picabia's saying "We have to be nomads, we have to traverse ideas the way we might traverse a village or a town."

To paraphrase the artist's words, the traversing of ideas always fosters the innovatory potential of knowledge. At Ducati in 1946 the idea to be traversed was called the Cucciolo.

"The motor-bicycle is part of the culture of the scooter," say Paolo Prato and Gianluca Trivero in *Viaggio e modernità*, "of which it is a variant in a pre-pubescent variant form. As such it belongs both to the sphere of transport and that of playthings. Speed is extraneous to it. The moped is a means of affirmation before being a means of transport, individual rather than collective. Like other 'mediatory technical pros-theses' (Virilio) which adolescents use in the effort to rec-oncile themselves to their own image and their developing bodies (radios, stereos, photographs), the moped bases a mythology of carefreeness on the exaltation of 'average' youthful values (school, friends, a certain good-hearted boisterousness, etc.). It belongs in the first place to the universe of gadgets. Its playful educative nature is given a prominent place in adverts, as in the following passage from a Piaggio catalogue: 'These easy-to-use vehicles will rejuvenate those who are no longer young and keep you if you still are. Youngsters like them because on the saddle they begin to feel like adults, while they learn to respect the traffic lights, give-way signs and the highway code' (Piaggio publicity catalogue). The moped seems to be most closely aligned with social trends claimed the two authors in the late 1980s. Just as the machine age changed the status of earlier forms of transport, turning them into objects of spectacle (like the horse), so the electronic era will turn cars, trains and boats into forms of entertainment (it has already happened at Disneyland), reserving transport to video-communications. This naturally according to the vision of McLuhan … The widespread and not immoderate pleasure of the moped resembles those big supersonic cocktail parties 30,000 feet above the Atlantic. In both the key word is discretion."

In Emilia Romagna they have a saying: the engine belongs to the motorcycle as the motorcycle belongs to the engine. The first half of the word itself, "motor," reasserts the quintes-

sence of the vehicle in question, its engine. At Ducati the Cucciolo evolved and shaped the motor-bicycle that then shed its pedals and turned into the light motorcycle. Then came the breakthrough: it was no longer a Cucciolo (cub), but a motorbike proper.

"The technical and social evolution of the motorcycle," continue Prato and Trivero, "followed an appreciably different course from other means of transport, with the partial exception of the truck. Though invented at the same time as the automobile, airplane and dirigible, which aroused the interest of the public and the media, the motorcycle came into its own only half a century later with the growth of youth movements and urban subcultures in the mid-nineteen-fifties."

It was in the later nineteen-fifties that Ducati made the breakthrough in design and production. "The epic of the motorcycle does not go back to the start of the century. Its splendors are not to be found in the decades between the wars, unlike many other forms of transport, and its vocabulary excludes words like 'luxury' and 'comfort.' Bourgeois culture never considered it capable of expressing any of its collective and individual myths, which it embodied in other vehicles. While the bicycle continued to live like a Cinderella

Cucciolo motor bicycles displayed by the Ducati concessionaire's in Bari.

among her more elegant sisters, the motorbike, the sidecar and the motor-bicycle were mainly working vehicles, or sport machines, or eccentric prostheses for a few exhibitionists (the rider in full biking gear who traverses the town like a meteor in Fellini's *Amarcord*)."

In a similar spirit, Ignazio Silone (1900–1978) in *Fontamara* describes the rare arrival of a motorbike in an even poorer part of provincial Italy, where it captivates and excites all the youngsters. "The electric light at Fontamara had likewise become something natural, like the moonlight. No one paid for it. No one had paid a bill in months. And what were we supposed to pay with? Recently the municipal bailiff no longer even came around to hand out the same old monthly bills for arrears, the same old bits of paper that we regularly used for our domestic purposes. The last time he called he was lucky to escape with his life. A charge of buckshot very nearly laid him low at the gates to the village. He had grown much more prudent. He would come to Fontamara when the men were at work and only the women and children at home. But you can't be too careful. He was very affable. He would hand out his bills with a pitiful, idiotic giggle and say, 'Take them, please. No need to get worked up. A scrap of paper always comes in handy around the house.' The electricity was scheduled to be cut off on January the first, then March the first. Then the first of May. Then people began saying: 'They won't cut it off now. It seems the Queen is against it. You'll see, they won't cut it off.' On June the first they finally did it. The women and children who were at home were the last to notice. But we men, coming back from work—those who had been to the mill and were coming back along the road, those who had been to the neighborhood of the cemetery and were coming back down the mountainside, those who had gone to the sandpit and were coming back along the canal, those who had been hired by the day and were coming back from all over the place—gradually, as darkness fell, saw the lights come on in the nearby villages while Fontamara grew blurred, hazy and shadowy, merging with the rocks, the thickets, the heaps of dung. We realized immediately what had happened. (It was and wasn't a surprise.) In fact the kids thought it was great fun. In our parts the kids don't get much of a chance for a bit of fun so when-

ever they do the poor creatures make the most of it. The same happens when a motorbike arrives, when two donkeys couple or a chimney catches fire."

In the nineteen-thirties and all through the nineteen-forties, explains Gian Franco Venè, "Even the motorbike races, which at that time covered hundreds of kilometers on grueling roads, seemed like horseplay compared with car racing. They lacked any particular merit, any glory worth the risk. It was observed that the smartest motorcycle riders moved into car racing as soon as they got the chance. The acrobats who exhibited themselves on motorbikes in fairgrounds, overcoming centrifugal force and chasing each other on the 'Wall of Death'—there would always be a girl among them in a leather suit and flowing blonde hair—aroused more pity than admiration. 'A death-defying ride every time,' the huckster would shout, while the blonde straddled a motorbike mounted on rollers and revved up the engine, her arms wide on the handlebars. 'Anything's better than hard work!' someone would invariably call out."

The urge to own and ride a motorbike certainly met with no encouragement in the family. "And if youngsters still living at home tried to make a breach in the family's commonsense," confirms Venè, "they would be repressed as delinquents and even interrogated: 'Who's put this wild idea in your head?' Many a friendship was cut short in this way.

The few youths who did ride up and down kitted out in racing gear every Sunday were looked on very suspiciously. 'Someone ought to ask him where he got the money from.' In the provinces they were all known by some unimaginative nickname they'd given themselves: 'Red Devil' or 'Black Panther' according to the color of the bike. On the rear fender or under the headlight they displayed the auspicious numbers 13 or 17, as if about to take part in a race. They wore leather jackets like the ones used by Allied aviators, with leggings, black crash helmets and leather ear muffs like cops in the Flying Squad. Around their necks they wore a scarf that fluttered behind them and gave an idea of speed."

Far from the great events of the history of the earlier twentieth century, roaring bikes shattered the quiet of the back blocks or pursued one another in hair-raising races along dusty roads. At village fairs the Wall of Death was the big attraction, exhibiting lusty blonde women in leather outfits on the saddles. It was only in the 1950s that motorbikes finally emerged from the gaudy painting of folklore and were ready to write their own epic.

"I had taken a degree in Political Science from Bologna, followed by a Master in International Marketing in London," recalls Marco Montemaggi. "Then I turned down offers of work in the field I'd majored in. I wanted to be a journalist and fulfill my natural urge to communicate. I was already writing for a number of papers with a nationwide circulation when, one morning in 1998, in my mailbox I found a letter with a ticket to a world Superbike competition. I had no experience of this world, but all the same I turned up at the Misano grandstand. I asked the young woman who wel-

comed me with a busy air why I had been invited. 'Federico Minoli wants to see you,' she said briskly. During the race I talked at some length with Federico, then newly appointed a director of Ducati, and his closing words were: 'You've got six months for research, a budget and two assistants. Tell me at once if it's a deal. Your job is to reconstruct the Ducati adventure from the war's end up to the present.' It was the chance to recount a legend and I could hardly refuse. I would get much experience in a field where I was a beginner. I accepted, perhaps led by my natural instinct (Italians from Emilia Romagna are said to be impulsive). I decided to reconstruct the Ducati path of design and production, going in search of the key models that above all others had signified excellence, the founders of whole families of bikes. The first of them was the Cucciolo in 1946. I realized I was going

The experience of pioneer racing mechanics blazed the trail for new specially designed frames.

to have a relatively easy job with production models and an extremely difficult one with racing bikes. Obviously it would not be hard to find examples of the former, but in the latter case perhaps just one model had been built and was now in the hands of a collector in another part of the world. I spent a week at Cinecittà (the big film studios in Rome), shut up in a projection room viewing period film clips and whole films of races on urban racing circuits as well as along the highways and byways. This confirmed that the former were mostly organized or promoted by concessionaires of the various makes. It was clear they had first intuited the value of racing to showcase the bikes' performance. It was a marketing tool for the products they would be putting on sale in their showrooms. But the latter kind of competition was clearly designed to promote tourism by road. The caravan of road racers took in towns, villages and hamlets that were no more than whistle stops for the railroads. Both kinds of races, however, provided information about the ruggedness and reliability of the engines and the setups of the bikes. They also fostered an urge to equal the feats of the riders, something that was open to everyone."

The races also confirmed the good mileage given by the Cucciolo and by micro-engines in general. This was no small matter in those years, which fostered the dream of the benefits to be had from industrial production.

"For the first time," states Ernesto Galli Della Loggia in *Italia contemporanea 1945/1975*, "Italians increasingly became familiar with mass-produced everyday objects. In many cases these people were still peasants, whose families had lived for centuries within a horizon of indigence made up of cheap objects, unvarying, colorless (think of the black that dominated clothing in the countryside) and lacking in imagination."

Among mass-produced products the Cucciolo offered freedom of movement, a low purchase price and economical running costs. All these features were guaranteed by the races, when the riders would talk to the spectators after some of their memorable feats.

A pioneer among the pioneers was Marco Recchia, a Ducati rider and mechanic in those years. He himself recounts his adventure: "Ducati took over the production rights for the Cucciolo from the SIATA firm in Turin, which had the license from Aldo Farinelli, a Turin lawyer who actually designed it in the first place. It was a one-cylinder four-stroke engine with a capacity of 48cc. We started production and I immediately decided to make a very special one-off version: I polished the valves, enlarged them, increased the compression ratio, mounted a bigger carburetor and added some other touches. I looked around for the frames best suited to racing. Then I went in for some short- and long-distance competitions and later, in 1951, I became the champion of Emilia Romagna. Between 1946 and the early fifties street races were held in practically all Italian cities. I remember Bari, Forlì, Bologna at the Margherita Gardens, the grounds of the Trade Fair in Milan. Then there were the long-distance races, like the grueling 1000-kilometer race from Milan to Taranto which I did twice. You lined up at midnight on the starting line at the Idroscalo (the old lake for flying boats in Milan) and then went hurtling down the boot of Italy all the way to the heel. I would stop to fill up in Florence and buy a little fruit for the journey. In Siena the engine went bust. I propped the Cucciolo against a bollard and changed a cotter pin. At this point I noticed the bearings were dilated by the heat. I had finished the grease so I mashed a banana to a paste and used it instead. I got as far as Rome, where I had to drop out. When racing I always tried to get the most out of the engine; it was the only way to go faster before the idea of fairing bikes for speed caught on. I tried to adopt the best position to cut through the air and protect myself from it, because racing was a cold business. I would stuff sheets of newspaper down my clothes and pedal like crazy whenever the slope strained the engine."

From Siena to Rome with mashed banana as a grease substitute. Truly exceptional, this bike specially prepared by Mario Recchia. The Poderosa II, by contrast, gave up the ghost and left Alberto Granada and Che Gavara stranded. "Alberto had a premonition and preferred not to drive," recounts Che, "so I took over. We went a few miles and stopped to fix the gears, which were playing up. Soon after, as we were taking a tight bend at fair speed, I braked and the butterfly screw flew off the rear brake. I grabbed the front brake-lever, which had been welded back on in makeshift fashion, and it snapped. For a few seconds all I saw were cows scattering in all directions while the poor Poderosa

Stunning victories in nearly all races meant Ducati concessionaires had little need to advertise its compact engines.

increased its velocity—we were going down a steep hill. The hoof of the last cow just grazed us by some miracle. All at once we saw we were heading for a nearby river that seemed to attract us with overwhelming force. I launched the bike against the embankment that skirted the road and we went bucking up it. A few yards further on we got wedged between two boulders. We dismounted and found ourselves unscathed. Though the accident hardly looked serious at first we soon realized our mistake. The motor played up strangely whenever we began to climb. Finally we tackled the Malleco rise: it has a railway bridge that the Chileans reckon the highest in the Americas. It was there that the bike gave up the ghost, making us waste the whole day waiting for some angel of mercy in the form of a truck to take us to the summit. That night we slept in the village of Cullipulli (after reaching our objective) and set off next morning fully expecting the catastrophe that threatened. At the first stiff climb—of the many on that road—La Poderosa sputtered to a halt."

The enthusiastic singer of the praises of the first Cucciolo,

designed as the T1 by SIATA and developed by Ducati, Mario Recchia was a mechanic for many long years at Borgo Panigale. There his racing experience was useful when it came to series production.

"In 1948 Ducati embarked on its first independent project, the T2. This was a development out of the T1," notes Marco Masetti, "and owed a lot to it. Changes were made to boost its power, make it more rugged and above all adapt it for production. The cylinder, for example, was redesigned (with changes to the fins) so that it slid out easily, since it was no longer incorporated in the timing case. This was totally redesigned so that the drive gears were easily accessible. The cylinder head was also altered so now it had the exhaust valve at the front, not at the back as in the T1. The power was increased by a quarter of a horsepower or rather more … The firm now offered (but only to order) a sport version of the T2 engine … Under the guidance of Giovanni Florio (then the Head Engineer) production

began on the T3, the first engine wholly designed by Ducati ... It had a 60cc engine ... In the war the Caproni firm at Rovereto had manufactured airplanes and flying boats. It was now seeking new outlets for production and in 1949 designed a special tubular frame with rear suspension (not just a modified bicycle frame) for the T3. The following year arrived the sport version of the 60cc engine. While the first version still had a frame with rear-wheel triangular suspension and a single shock-absorber, the second one had swinging forks and two pairs of telescopic shock absorbers. When Caproni pulled out (to manufacture motorcycles under its own name), Ducati commissioned new frames with even closer affinities to a motorcycle, partly because the successive versions of the T3 had boosted performance. The Cucciolo T3 engines developed technically in various sizes (50, 55, 60, 65cc) and the series continued into the late nineteen-fifties."

The dynamic of this process is quite clear. First came the production and sale of a micro-engine kit for application to a bicycle; then the experiences of pioneer racers, who were also mechanics, pointed the way to specially designed frames and a gradual increase in cylinder size leading up to the light motorcycle. Everything at Ducati was now tending toward the design of a motorbike proper. The Cucciolo had now won almost every race, with a record number of entries in events between 1948 and 1951, many crowned with victories. In 1949 it took the first five positions at the Nighttime Gymkhana in Siena.

"I'll take you on my Cucciolo." By this time several thousand users had used it and thousands more would soon do so. As the song said: "Il motorino è piccolo/ ma batte come il mio cuor. / Per monti e per città/ andremo velocissimi/ uniti e felicissimi …" Its stunning victories in almost every race meant the Ducati concessionaires had little need to promote either the kit for application to a bicycle or the version mounted on a special frame, with a markedly sporty styling.

Mario Recchia took part in short and long-range races and was champion of Emilia Romagna in 1951.

But as the 1950s wore on these one-cylinder engines gradually lost their attraction. This became clear above all in big national races like the Motogiro, the Mille Miglia for motorbikes and the even more legendary Milan-Taranto race. People would throng the highroads and byroads to catch a fleeting glance of the riders, who set amazing new speed records. Only bikes with a big engine capacity could now achieve this. So now Ducati saw the need to ride the tiger, or so at least thought Giuseppe Montano.

Marco Musetti picks up the story: "Ducati's General Manager, Dr. Montano, certainly picked a winner when, in 1954, he hired a young engineer from Lugo di Romagna, Fabio Taglioni.

Taglioni came from the Mondial firm, where he was eclipsed by several other engineers who had already succeeded in making a name for themselves. They were jealous of Taglioni, who had designed and built a fine 75cc racing bike with the help of his pupils at a Technical Institute and then ceded the design to the Ceccato company."

Taglioni turned over

his 75cc bike to the most determined entrepreneur of the day. "Pietro Ceccato," notes Marta Boneschi in *Poveri ma belli*, "began his career as a pharmacist but was then swept away by his passion for engines. He was one of those people who don't stop at new plant, new products and new markets. He wanted to go further and pioneer new methods of management. In 1953 his engineering works at Alte Montecchio on the outskirts of Vicenza manufactured bicycles, motorbikes, compressors, gas cylinders and plant for service stations. He had about 600 employees, who managed to save 14 million man-hours in just one year at parity of production by contributing hundreds of different ideas for saving time, money and labor. Ever since the firm launched the slogan 'Use your head to produce' everyone would lend a hand, testifies the foreman Gentilin. 'No one had ever asked me to say what I thought about my job. Then one day

they did ask, so I suggested a new way of painting the bikes.'" An interesting demonstration of the way entrepreneurial enthusiasm can help boost the firm's output.

At Ducati, notorious for its shaky management, there was a very different climate when the young Taglioni accepted the invitation held out by Dr. Montano, who claimed to be the first executive positively interested in producing motorcycles.

"Taglioni had a passion for racing and fine engineering," confirms Marco Masetti, and from his first days at Ducati he tried to leave his mark on production. The choice fell on a 100cc single-cylinder engine with overhead cam and bevel drive capable of very high speeds. This arrangement (which turns up most of Taglioni's bikes) was considered difficult to build and expensive unless you had good machinery and first-rate workmen. There was no problem at Ducati, which gave him carte blanche. The result was the Gran Sport 100, better known as the Marianna."

A big dog with long white fur comes up to the gate, barking and wagging its tail. Then all at once it turns around and runs up the short ramp that rises from the garden to the upper floor of Taglioni's house at Bologna. His wife Norina stands in the doorway of their spacious living room and smilingly calls to the dog, who is again barking and wagging his tail at the gate. Reassured by the presence of our hostess we go in. Livio Lodi has already explained to me that a visit to Fabio Taglioni should be undertaken in the spirit of a pilgrimage to a shrine. Norina ushers us in. "At this hour," (three o'clock on a stifling afternoon), "my husband has his nap. I've spent all these long years at his side and the history of his achievements is part of my life."

She begins her story: "It was when Fabio was still working for Mondial and was putting the last touches to the 175cc, his latest brainchild. He had already won races with his earlier engines. One day Dr. Giuseppe Montano, Ducati's

Fabio Taglioni designs
the GS100 in 1954.
"Fabio said: 'I've accepted
a challenge and I've got
to win.'"
Norina Taglioni

Director General, called him up with an urgent plea: 'We need a win in the higher classes. You've got to design a 100cc bike capable of winning the Motogiro, otherwise this firm will be on the rocks.' 'Is that meant as a challenge to me?' asked Fabio. 'Why not see it as challenge to yourself?' 'I accept.' This brief conversation in late 1953 decided our future. Fabio came home and I showed him a letter we'd just received from Ford, asking him to move to Detroit. The letter was accompanied by a contract with the figure left blank, to be filled in at Fabio's discretion. I never tried to influence my husband's decisions, not even then! The idea of going to America! Fabio said: 'I've accepted a challenge and I've got to win it. We'll go to America some other time, Norina.' For the next month I hardly saw anything of him. Night and day he was at Ducati, busy with draftsmen, mechanics, frame-designers, until the engine was run on the test bed and did everything he expected of it. The running assembly was built around it and the team moved to Latina for trials. The 100cc went into production because at that time you couldn't race a prototype, you had to have some production models. Meanwhile my husband asked Dr. Montano for leave so he could spend some days at Mondial and put the finishing touches to the 175cc. It was as if that engine was his child and he wanted to teach it to walk. We met up in Rome on New Year's Eve, at a café, because I didn't want to spend the festive season alone in Bologna. Finally it was the day of the Motogiro and the big race. This was a marathon run in stages. The first leg started from under the two towers and then the whole circus traveled north before returning to Bologna for the final leg. The race ended at Porta Santo Stefano, where a grandstand was erected. There I sat next to a woman who kept crying out 'O God! Oh God!' and praying, 'Make him go slow, I mean fast, now he's winning!' and so on, contradicting herself at every breath. In fact the news had just come over the radio that Giovanni Degli Antoni, her son, was

"Marianna they called it at Ducati, after Mary, because Dr. Montano's wife was a devotee of the Madonna." *Norina Taglioni*

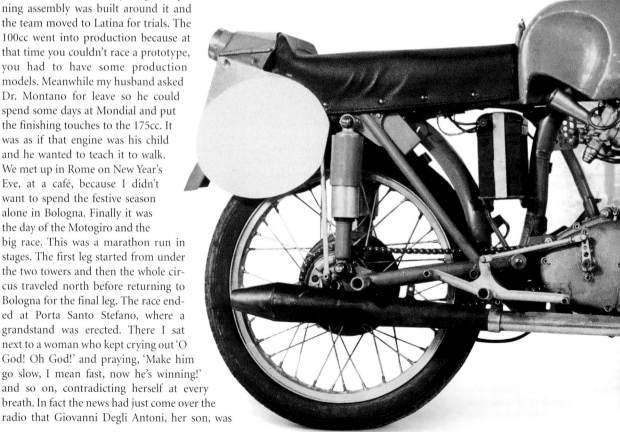

leading the race on a Ducati 100cc. Soon after we saw him come racing in at the head of the field, going like the wind. In the delirium of general joy over the victory I saw Fabio at last. He was in a pitiful state, thinner than ever, his face gaunt and drawn. 'What's wrong?' I asked. He said he'd been feverish in Rome and the doctors ordered him to his hotel bed. He had already followed every stage of the Motogiro in a car and had no intention of missing the final leg. He leapt out of bed, hollering that if they didn't let him go he'd shoot the lot of them— he'd never owned a gun in his life … And all because of the 100cc.

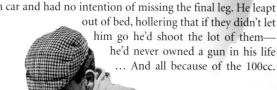

Marianna they called it at Ducati, after Mary, because Dr. Montano's wife was a devotee of the Madonna."

Norina Taglioni's story provides a vivid sketch of Taglioni's impulsive Romagnolo character. Feeling slighted at Mondial he showed his resoluteness. He immediately quit his job and accepted Ducati's challenge to design and build a winning bike in record time.

"The story goes," recounts Marco Montemaggi, "that at the end of a race where his bikes had swept the board, Taglioni was inexplicably, perhaps intentionally, overlooked when invitations went out for the party at Mondial. It may have been envy on the part of the big shots. Taglioni never thought twice: he packed his bags and cleared out the same day. Perhaps this was why he wanted to be there despite his temperature, to celebrate Degli Antonio's victory on his legendary Marianna, the 100cc bike that brought renown to Ducati. He wanted the people at Mondial to know that engine packed all the power of his wrath."

Taglioni reasserted the primacy of the engine as the quintessence of the motorcycle. Taglioni's engines *were* Ducati bikes, just as Ducati bikes were Taglioni, and this remained true for another thirty years from that magical 100cc of 1954. By contrast, in the world of four wheels, it was two great car designers that rescued the fortunes of another firm

Giovanni Degli Antoni,
wins the 1955 Motogiro
on a GS100.

in those same years as, like Ducati, it struggled in the toils of state ownership. I myself wrote for *Abitare*: "It was Nuccio Bertone's Giulietta Sprint in 1954 and Pinin Farina's Giulietta Spider in '55 that revived confidence and pride at Alfa Romeo. They also gave Bertone and Pininfarina a chance to break out of a purely craft dimension of design and assembly into mass-producing the Sprint and Spider *fuorieserie* for Alfa Romeo. At one step they developed into big manufacturers by enlarging market niches that the large car companies could never have exploited.

There was an even more curious episode: these two fine sports machines preceded the birth of a sports sedan, the Berlina Giulietta. Alfa Romeo was to begin production in 1956. A unique case in the history of motor manufacturing, as G.B. Panicco confirms: 'The Alfa Romeo company, in the person of Rudolf Hruska, had vowed to shareholders that Alfa Romeo would bring out a completely new sports sedan in the very near future. Realizing he risked betraying their trust in him, he turned to Bertone to make good his promise. A draw was held and a lucky few of the subscribers received not the new sedan but the first Giulietta Sprints, of which Bertone eventually built no fewer than forty thousand over an arc of ten years. The studies began in 1953, but the prototype was presented at the Turin Motor Show in spring of '54. In the prototype the front shield masking the air intake and surmounted by the badge was much larger than in the production model. The chrome bars at the sides, including the sidelights, were set closer together and more elongated toward the point of the shield. The rear window was incorporated in the trunk, but because of problems over making the presses this design was discarded in favor of two separate pieces…'"

So the Giulietta Sprint was the big break that enabled Bertone to expand his design shop into an industrial concern. Much the same happened with Pinin Farina and the Spider.

"My father," recalls his son Sergio, "was convinced that only series production could fully confirm the validity of a design. This was the reason behind our expansion. Alfa Romeo's American importer, Hoffman Motor Car Inc. in New York, pressed the firm to produce a sports car with quintessential Italian styling to compete with the Jaguar XK150, Mercedes 190SL, MG A and Triumph TR 3, the models that then dominated this particular niche in the States. The fact that the same models were also dominant in Europe made us feel we should have our say, so we tooled up for series production. The presses cost a lot compared with the traditional method of a panel-beater shaping the pieces on a wooden model, but they ensured absolute precision in the components we turned out. Once they were in place and working the presses turned out absolutely identical hoods and fenders. Of course the firm needed a guaranteed production run to offset the big investment and the Giulietta Spider, with thirty thousand cars turned out in a few years, fully justified the conversion. The 1954 version had a very advanced wraparound windshield and manufacturing it at once proved difficult.

FIAT *la Seicento*
Illustrazione tecnica della nuova vettura Fiat
la piccola 4 posti economica

KLUZER-MILANO
C. SEMPIONE 37

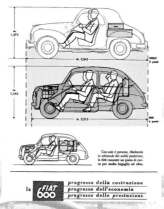

ALLA 600 (4 POSTI)

la **FIAT 600** progresso della costruzione
progresso dell'economia
progresso delle prestazioni

We opted for a more restrained form that was easier to produce using techniques then available. It also had the advantage of being lighter and esthetically very elegant. The bumper guards were designed very high for better protection but they were hard to press. We cut them back, which also improved the visual impact. The rear lights were aligned according to the government regulations. In 1955 we began production of the Giulietta Spider, *la bella signorina* as my father dubbed it, to distinguish it from the more celebrated sedan, the queen of the road …"
While designer-entrepreneurs Nuccio Bertone and Pinin Farina were trans-

forming the excellent mechanicals of the Alfa Romeo Giulietta into the splendid configurations of the Sprint and Spider, the song of the engines designed by the Romagnolo Fabio Taglioni gave a voice to Ducati bikes worldwide and impressed his hallmark on the pure engineering tradition of Borgo Panigale's reds.

In his *Viaggio in Italia* Guido Piovene (1907–1974) surveyed the character of the inhabitants of Emilia Romagna: "I listen to some Bolognese folk discussing the cities of Emilia Romagna and their different characters. They say: 'Parma is gentle, humorous, culture-loving, with a touch of nostalgia for the female paternalism of Marie Louise. Reggio is cordial, generous, active, and its interest in history is more cultural than patriotic. Modena is inward-looking, technical, tenacious, but humorless, and a bit on the prickly side. Never confuse humor with wisecracking or slapstick, the Bolognese cautioned. The same goes for Ferrara: that's why political conflicts are ruthless there, with no quarter given. Romagna, my Bolognese friends declare, is tough, uncompromising …"
In Fabio Taglioni these traits took the form of a determined, visceral passion for his work, where the man was one with the legend of the solitary, inspired designer.
Guido Piovene's portrait continues: "Hedonistic, easygoing, humorous: that's how the Bolgonese see Bologna. The passion for politics is a true passion, a vital tension, an aspect of their love of life, a part of their sensuousness, their physical appetite, their veneration of virility. And finally it is part of their optimism, which springs from the very richness of their sanguine humors, and achieves renewal in total redemption …"

The legend of the Romagnolo Taglioni blends with this background and is fueled by another passion that in Bologna is truly a passion: the love of engines.

"When pointy shoes were all the fashion," continues Piovene, "young people in Bologna wore shoes almost as long as skis. One young fellow, who wore them longer than anyone else, became the founder of a school. There is a man there who always dresses in a *bersagliere* uniform. He strolls about under the porticoes, his chest swathed with medals, quite possibly false, marches at the head of all the processions and wants to hobnob with all the visiting ministers. There are inspired autodidacts, often true geniuses. The merchants, tall and portly, wearing long black cloaks, push forward to sell in the heart of the city. Sport divides the citizens into factions, reviving a spirit of parochial rivalry with Ferrara and Modena, reflecting the legacy of the ancient wars between city states. The motorcycle dominates. It is the great plaything of the Emilian plains: every city or village has its 'Sport Café,' where youths stand on the threshold, vying for a ride on a new motorbike and all the talk is about crazy speeds…"

In *Cara Italia* Giuseppe Raimondi (1898–1985) describes the speech that embodies the distinctive character of the Emilians: "I suppose other regions have a character and language of their own. We Emilians have ours. Men talk the way nature, things, the successive strata of things and human events, have taught them. Speech rises to the lips in harmony with the cadences of the heart, the laws of custom, and the character of every living being. They shape it and give it sound and meaning. So the speech of every different language is colored with the colors of material things, and even of the sky, that lie around and above on all sides. The language of the Emilians is neither sweet nor delicate in its tones, but it is limpid, emphatic and precise, as if a light shed by the place and the way of life had entered into soul of the people. It has its barbaric roots, its ancient and invincible word-endings: but this is a historical law that, like the weapons, the violence and the categories of thought, it has accepted immersing them within themselves …"

In the years he spent with Ducati Fabio Taglioni accentuated the color of the "barbaric roots, the ancient and invincible word-endings," translating them into the sound of his invincible engines. In

Bologna the architecture of engines excites all the senses, rather like the culinary hyperbole to which Piovene inevitably succumbs: "The Bolognese dish is the apotheosis of the Baroque still life. In one restaurant, which I entered by chance, I asked for some roast meat. They set before me a dish of pheasant, wild duck, some other water fowl, I can't remember what else, plus wild boar and hare, with a whole thrush topping off the entire construction. Cesarina, a celebrated Bolognese hostess, if this classic word hostess doesn't sound offensive, says to me: 'While you're wait-

ing for the minestra I think I'll give you a little consommé.' She brings me an appetizer of tortellini in beef broth. I say feebly that all I wanted was some consommé. 'Bolognese consommé is what you've got in front of you,' Cesarina says. 'You can't call those things swimming in it tortellini. Why, there's no more than thirty of them.' Having expounded this theory of tortellini as an ingredient of consommé she relates the myth of their ori-

in America, Spaggiari took part in numerous races and was repeatedly victorious, which is all the more stunning if you think of the troubles Ducati had in those years."

As Marco Masetti notes: "In 1949 began the hapless administration of the bankruptcy receiver Mantelli, followed by more careful management by the *avvocato* Stoppato, who divided the industrial activities (concentrated mainly at the Borgo Panigale works) into three distinct sections: engineering, electro-technical and optical. The future, however, remained uncertain because of continual labor disputes and picketing outside the factory. In 1953 the firm was further split into two distinct joint-stock companies: Ducati Meccanica (engineering) and Ducati Elettrotecnica (electro-technicals)." They diverged widely and the latter split again into the present Ducati Elettronica, with its headquarters in Bologna, and Ducati Radiotelecomunicazioni now based in Milan. They have no connection with Ducati Motor, the present denomination of Ducati Meccanica.

"From the very start," continues Marco Masetti, "the GS100 was the bike to beat in the long-distance trials as well as being the battlehorse of more than one generation

gin: it seems that in ancient times the host of a tavern peeped through a keyhole and saw Venus naked, so he took the opportunity to copy her navel. Seventeenth-century cuisine and mythology. Bolognese tortellini disdain comparison with tortellini from other parts of Emilia Romagna: they differ not only in shape but also in the quality of the filling. Someone else describes the feast at a country wedding. Hams and salami, tortellini, then many-layered lasagna pies stuffed with truffles; cheese and sausage-meat arrayed on trays as broad as the tables: each diner carves himself a brick-sized portion. Then zamponi (stuffed pig's trotters) and boiled meats, songbirds served on a bed of polenta, and roast meats. The Bolognese sweet pastries are broad, full-bellied, creamy, vaguely suggestive of an advanced pregnancy…"

Riding a motorbike means hugging the body of the machine to your body, bonded by movement. The rite fulfills the integration between pulsating forms that exchange their heat: animal warmth and the heat generated by whirring metal. Hence the likeness of rider and bike to the mythical centaurs, half man, half horse, conceived when Ixion sacrilegiously embraced a cloud molded by Zeus into the shape of Hera.

"The Marianna won everything everywhere: the Motogiro of 1954 to '57," recites Marco Montemaggi, "two editions of the Milan-Taranto; Farnè rode it in Spain;

"On Friday November 30, 1956, forty-four world records were shattered on the speed ring of the Monza track."
Luigi Bianchi, Marco Masetti

of riders worldwide. But Taglioni was not just a great engineer with a passion for racing bikes. He saw clearly that his engines and motorcycles had to be developed into production models. So, keeping to the basic concept of the Marianna series, he devised a sequence of road bikes that began to win a worldwide public. Presented with engines ranging from 125 to 250cc, in tourist and sport versions, the Ducatis were esteemed in the United States, where they were pushed by the Berliner Brothers, the importers for North America."

1958, Elite 200
Two mufflers were stacked
across the rear wheel and
the power unit was topped
by a voluminous fuel tank,
with an elongated design
that gave the whole machine
a rakish look.

Ducati used the racing career of the Cucciolo to publicize the quality of the production model of its micro-engine, a perfect marketing operation sturdily supported by Ducati's concessionaires. Every season they organized reliability trials to promote the Cucciolo. This was not an attempt to conquer a market niche but to extend its horizons. The legendary Marianna had thrilled the crowds thronging the roads for the Motogiro and the Milan-Taranto race. Speed buffs formed a pool of potential customers whom Ducati had to satisfy by finally producing a real motorcycle and so keep up with its competitors in Italy and abroad, who were already prepared to meet the demand.

Taglioni decided to translate the dream of the many into a reality for the few: in 1958 he designed and built a production model, the Elite 200. There is a curious disparity here: unlike a blood stallion, put out to stud after a string of dazzling victories in the hope that his favored genes will reappear in his offspring, Marianna was a thoroughbred who never went out to grass, continued racing and collecting victories while giving birth to many road bikes.

"Elite was designed with the Italian market in mind but had a broad appeal for bikers worldwide," write Luigi Bianchi and Marco Masetti in "Motociclismo racconta la storia della Ducati." "They were

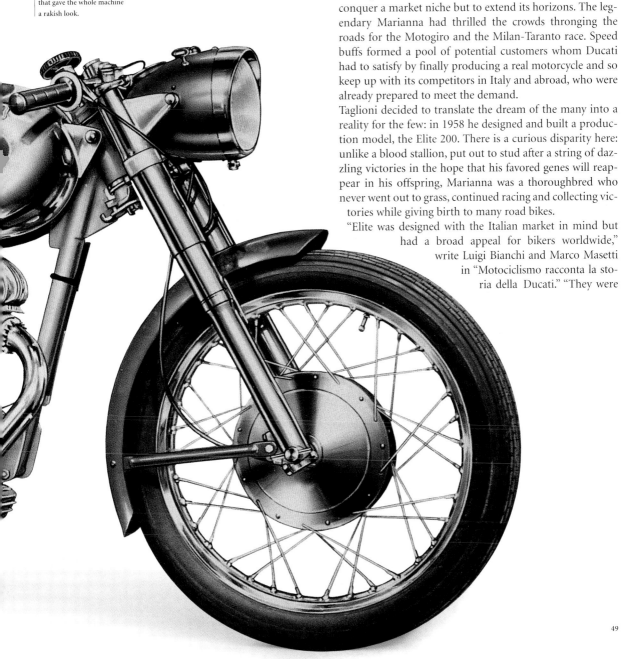

attracted by the marque's fame from its many racing victories. The engine was clearly a bigger version of the well-known 175 and was described as 'simple and sturdy.' Riding it was immensely enjoyable, as confirmed by its top speed of 140 kmh, which was notable for the period. And yet it was not a model with explicit sport ambitions but rather a bike that would perform well whatever the occasion."

With the Marianna's debut in 1955 Fabio Taglioni had met the need for a racing machine; in 1958, with the Elite 200, he met the need for an all-round bike for everyday use. The two models differed in scope: the first was a racing bike, the second a road bike, and they appealed to different sets of users: the first to racing riders, the second to bikers who formed the most loyal market niche.

"If your first experience of motors was on a Guzzi, a Gilera or a Ducati, or on the saddle of a Laverda, a Motom, a gentle Galletto or a terrible Bianchi Sparviero, then you'll never resign yourself to the comfort of an automobile," notes Marta Boneschi, "the stability of four wheels or the absence of the wind blowing in your face."

Bikers had nothing in common with the *scooteristi*, who in that period were soon to move on from two to four wheels. They were and still are a class apart. Motorcycles are not meant as a convenient way of getting about, they're meant to procure emotions of the kind you can't do without. So motorbikes have a lot of the gadget about them, and in this sense they are not a *means* of transport, they'll never take over the vehicle market, they'll always be a niche for modes of being. The biker may use a car sometimes, but he'll choose the motorbike as a style of life and he'll keep riding, however rarely, because he's hopelessly besotted with it.

DUCATI
200 élite

4 stroke
200 cc.

Timing by O.H.C.
Gearbox 4 speeds.

Maximum speed Km/h 135 (Ml/h 83.534).

Fuel consumption lt. 3.4 per 100 Kms (81 Ml/imp. gal. = 69 Ml/US gal.).

ENGINE - Single-cylinder - Bore: 67 mm. - Stroke: 57.8 mm. - Displacement 203.783 cc. - Compression ratio: 7.8 : 1 - Timing by O.H.C. valves inclined 80° - Maximum output: HP 18 - Maximum revs. per minute 7,500 - Cooling by air - Lubrication: forced by gear pump - Oil sump in crankcase - Ignition by distributor - Sparking plug: Marelli CW 260 N - Electrical equipment: Battery fed - Battery recharged by means of an alternator-flywheel and rectifier - Three-light headlamp - Tail light with Stop - Horn - Transmission: from engine to gearbox, by gears: from gearbox to wheel, by chain with special cushion drive - Gearbox: in unit with engine - 4 speeds: gears in constant mesh; pedal control with preselector - Clutch: multi-plate disc running in bath of oil.

FRAME - Highly resistant steel tubing. Built on smart lines - Front suspension: telehydraulic fork complete with steering dampers - Rear suspension: swinging fork with adjustable hydraulic shock absorbers - Wheels: spoke type; chromium steel rims with special Sport profile; 18''×2½'' - Brakes: expanding: front, hand operated; rear, brake foot - Drum diameter: front, 180 mm.; rear, 160 mm. - Tyres: 2,75-18; front, ribbed; 3,00-18 with block tread, the rear.

Weight (unladen) . . . . Kg. 111 (lbs. 244.710)
Oil sump holds approx . . Kg. 2 (lt. 2.400 = lbs. 4.409)
Fuel tank holds . . . . . lt. 17 (Imp. gal. 3.3796 = US gal. 4.4909)

DUCATI MECCANICA S.p.A. - P.O.B. 313 - PHONE: 49.16.01 - BOLOGNA (ITALY)

STUDIO LUCY - LITOGRAFIA SCHIASSI - BOLOGNA   PRINTED IN ITALY

Figlia della GS100, a differenza della mitica Marianna, Elite 200 si commisura all'uso comune, che è pur sempre quello del mezzo che permette di conseguire emozioni irripetibili.

"One day in 1955"—the Marianna was now flying to repeated victories and Fabio Taglioni must already have had the Elite 200 in mind—recalls Gianfranco Venè, "the main roads in Turin were cleared to allow the triumphal passage of an array of beige, white and blue motor cars with unpredictable styling and dimensions. Like the motor scooter nine years earlier, the Fiat 600 rolling off President Vittorio Valletta's assembly lines were pulverizing the tradition that the underprivileged should content themselves with a pretentious little car, cheap and comfortable only in appearance, like the Fiat 500, popularly called the 'Topolino' ('Mickey Mouse car'). The Fiat 600 was not, or at least it did not look like, half a car palmed off on people who could not afford a whole one. The engine did not pull it but pushed. At the front, instead of a radiator grid it had a simple molding. To start it you simply flicked a switch next to the seat; the dashboard looked like a mantelpiece clock; the doors opened backward. There was ample space for four people; luggage went into a compartment at the front. So there was no point in comparing it to the Fiat 500 A, B, C or Giardinetta (station wagon). But if you persisted in making the comparison, you had to concur that in the hierarchy of motorcars the 600 was much more powerful, spacious and speedy than the old Topolino, and so it was a step up the social ladder at a price of 590,000 lire, payable in easy installments, much less than the 500 five years earlier, when the motor scooter was already a big step forward … On the eve of the postwar boom hundreds of thousands of ordinary men and women became car-owners, well aware they were not clumsily imitating the wealthy and quite clear about the distance between themselves and those condemned to riding on two wheels. The Fiat 600 brought a new word into the Italian language, the feminine adjective-cum-noun *utilitaria*, which ever since has denoted the difference between this kind of automobile and other cars, large or small: it is utilitarian…"

As for the price, now competitive and by maximum correspondence to its function, the *utilitaria* in those years certainly confined the enthusiasts of the Elite 200 and other leading Italian and foreign models. "The *utilitaria*," continues Gian Franco Venè, "was accepted, even welcomed at the firm, because it guaranteed punctuality. Proud new owners would invite their colleagues to look out the office window at where it was parked among other identical models but distinguished by the unrepeatable glossiness of recent delivery … A tacit pact established that

the step up from the *utilitaria* would not precede promotion: the 600 (or the new Fiat 500 of 1957, costing less than 500,000 lire), would do up to the level of office manager. From office manager to the near-executive levels came the Fiat 1100, including the two-tone 1100L (for luxury), or else the Lancia Appia, rather more classy but still a middle-range car. With the key to the executive washroom all the way up to the top management the choice of car was free: in this—only in this, note—ours is a traditional firm. For the rest we were very advanced. But you're intelligent, you've caught my meaning … The treacherous fascination of car-ownership lost its power, it ended up confined to the outer cities, while the freedom already savored on a motor scooter overflowed into broader spaces. The statistics began to show that the car had

Your first impression of the Elite 200 was a sense of safety.

DUCATI raccomanda carburanti e lubrificanti ESSO
di **EXTRA** *non c'è che* **ESSO**

1961, Scrambler
The 250cc version fulfilled
the dream of Ducati lovers
across the Atlantic,
even before it was marketed
in Europe.

become a means of work or pleasure, a love nest …"

For the first time the automobile, especially the *utilitaria*, enlarged the range of its functions and became a multipurpose, protected space, to be personalized by its owner: "Between lovers, the *utilitaria* became a common good, like the hideout it was driven to. 'Our Carolina,' they called it affectionately, 'our hideaway.' The range of little birthday presents was extended to include the knick-knacks that cluttered the windows of accessory shops: a cover for the steering wheel, a fancy knob for the gearshift, a can of paint to color the tire-walls white, a key-ring with an ivory skull, a rag doll to hang from the rear-vision mirror, a chrome or imitation leather ashtray with a magnet that stuck to the dashboard, a framed picture of St. Christopher with room for a small photograph, cord half-gloves for sporty driving, the Touring Club's road maps showing the latest *autostrade*."

The *autostrade*, the new expressways, were to be the deputed place of car traffic, while the motorbikes weaved expertly between their roaring hoods. "On the Touring Club's road maps, published on the eve of the 1960s, the peninsula was traversed by broken yellow lines that indicated the *autostrade* then under construction. After a stretch joining Milan and Parma the broken line dribbled down toward Rome, formed a little pool around it and then headed on toward Naples. On the very edge of Milan, one day in 1956, the authorities civil and military inaugurated a plain white marble pillar. The sides bore, in bronze lettering, the word ORIGIN and on the front: AUTOSTRADA OF THE SUN—MILAN—BOLOGNA—FLORENCE—ROME—NAPLES. When you get in the car you're in northern Italy, you close door and before you know it you're in the south…"

Here the turnpike really marked the difference, it feared no comparisons: night or day, cold, rain or blazing heat, the cars could always travel.

The Elite 200 had nothing to do with the phenomenon of mass car ownership, it was a thoroughbred, an object of veneration on the part of those who loved speed on two wheels, those who call each other *Ducatisti*. Taglioni had skillfully kindled their enthusiasm. "Only in the heyday of Italian motorbiking," noted Luigi Bianchi and Marco Masetti, "could it happen that two rival riders, Mario Carini and Santo Ciceri, set forty-odd world speed records using a machine that was practically identical to the one used in traditional races, with the help of modest support from the manufacturer. On Friday, November 30, 1956, forty-four world records were shattered on the speed ring of the Monza track. Thirteen were in the 100cc class, another thirteen in the 125, and yet another thirteen in the 175…"

Again in that magic 1956: "Traversing the Po valley covered in snow," continue Bianchi and Masetti, "the then director of *Motociclismo*, Arturo Coerezza, and the promising young journalist Carlo Perelli, defied the weather and reached the factory…"

At Borgo Panigale Taglioni had developed a new racing engine, derived from the 100cc by revolutionizing the drive: a one-cylinder, twin cam, 125cc engine capable of turning over at 11,500 revs. "Patently derived from the Gran Sport

Joe Berliner, left, who pushed the idea of the Scrambler in the States.

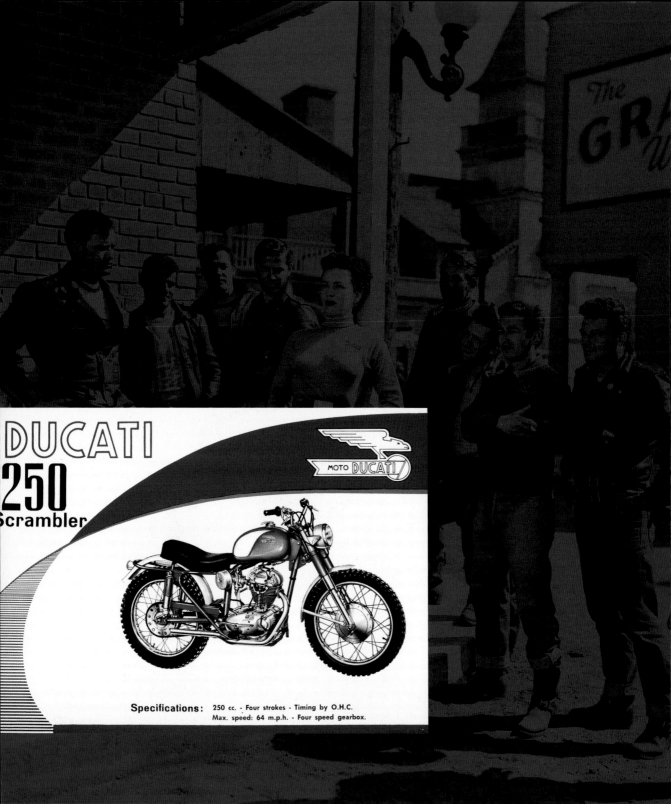

DUCATI
250
SCRAMBLER

O.H.C. 4 stroke **5** speeds foot shift

BERLINER MOTOR CORPORATION
Railroad Street and Plant Road,
Hasbrouck Heights, New Jersey - U.S.A

DUCATI MECCANICA S.p.A. - CAS. POST. 313 - PHONE: 40.02.50 - BOLOGN
PRINTED

hubs. The line of the flanks linked front and rear; the play for maneuvering was indicated by the molding near the position of the arms. The design cut down on air resistance but made steering more awkward and forced the rider into a cramped position.

In 1957 Taglioni evolved the 125cc into a triple cam desmo model. Bianchi and Masetti report his observation on this: "The principal aim is to compel the valve to follow faithfully the diagram of distribution, while the saving in energy dispersal is almost negligible … It makes performance more consistent and reliable."

The victories of the new thoroughbreds inflamed the hearts of the *Ducatisti*. The first bike, the twin-cam won the 1956 Swedish Grand Prix and with Grandossi in 1958 the Italian Senior Title; the same rider missed victory by a whisker in the World Championship. The triple-cam's honors list included absolute

DUCATI
250-350 SCRAMBLER

O.H.C. 4 stroke **5** speeds foot shift

that dominated the Motogiro and the Milan-Taranto races, the twin cam was mounted on a racing assembly that was substantially the same as its progenitor, with the simple cradle frame open below…"

The front fender, partly faired, prevented the danger of lift at high speeds. The splendid windshield capped the fuel tank and hugged its sides. The tank itself, long and sinuous on the lower side, enhanced the architecture of the engine. The rider's seat was set well toward the tail. Even at a standstill the streamlined good looks made it seem as if it was moving and the effect was truly stunning. The 100cc, at Monza, had an aluminum alloy fairing that covered the whole machine, so that in profile it looked as if a pair of shears had been used to cut the driver's seat out of the bodywork, which then continued below the

BERLINER MOTOR CORPORATION
Railroad Street and Plant Road,
Hasbrouck Heights, New Jersey - U.S.A.

DUCATI MECCANICA S.p.A. - CAS. POST. 313 - 40100 BOLOGNA - ITALIA - TEL. 40.02.50
printed in italy

"The concept of the 'motorcycle outlaw' was uniquely American."
Hunter S. Thompson

The Cult film *The Wild One* embedded the myth in the collective imagination.

The Scrambler shares none of that untamed passion for racing of *Ducatisti* worldwide.

domination of its category in 1958; in Monza, in the Gran Prix of the Nations, Ducati machines took the first five places. Then in 1958 the Elite 200 was presented to passionate motorcyclists as the summa of experience, developed and proven on the racetracks, a bike of tried and tested reliability.

The offspring of the GS100, unlike its sisters and the mythical Marianna, the Elite 200, was designed for everyday use but it also promised incomparable emotions. The Elite extended Ducati's market niche well beyond Italy to include the whole biking world. The first impression it gave you was a sense of safety. The details of its architecture reinforced this conviction: the cradle frame, tele-forks, rear suspension with a swinging fork and two telehydraulic shock absorbers. Across the middle of the rear wheel there were two superimposed mufflers, while the power unit showed off its 90 liter specific horsepower, surmounted by the fuel tank, which was voluminous but its elongated design gave a rakish look to the whole machine. The saddle clasped the rear fender and projected without a break over the lower side of the tank.

The Elite 200 appealed not just to the solitary rider: it enabled the biker to share the thrill with someone else. Don't be afraid, cling to me and "we'll go fast, we'll be happy," went the Cucciolo refrain in 1946. In '58, with the Elite, speed truly became the accomplice of the happy moment, of the close and impassioned embrace when the passenger was your sweetheart. Quite unlike the traditional couple, who misted over the windows of their *utilitaria* parked in some discreet place at night: they clasped in the roar of the engine, which played its melody at the end of an evening spent dancing to rock and roll.

"The motorbike—freedom, transgression, an

DUCATI

450 SCRAMBLER

O.H.C. 4 stroke **5** speeds foot shift

SOLE U. S. DISTRIBUTOR

BERLINER MOTOR CORPORATION

Railroad Street and Plant Road, Hasbrouck Heights, New Jersey - U. S. A.

printed in Italy

anomalous, precarious way to travel," note Prato and Trivero, "and rock and roll—the return of the body to music—embodied a youth culture that was just emerging after decades of latency dominated by tradition. Motorbikes and automobiles were freed from that functionalist ethic that saw them as above all practical vehicles: they became inscribed in a hedonism of wandering founded on the repetition of ritual gestures, on driving around town, traveling without going anywhere."

Rebel Without a Cause (1955) by Nicholas Ray, a cult film of the period, created the myth of young people mutinying against family restrictions, work, the intransigent moralism of the society they lived in. That myth has a name: James Dean, the sad-eyed rebel, Jim Stark in the fiction. An only child, growing up in a family that has always cherished him, Jim has no apparent reason for rebelling. Yet he rejects the care lavished on him, considering it purely conventional, and hungers for authenticity. The love of Judy (Natalie Wood) and the friendship of Plato (Sal Mineo) seem to fulfill his existential needs. But Judy is the girl of a rival gang-leader (Corney Allen), and they play chicken. Their cars are launched at speed toward a cliff edge and the loser is the one who jumps first. Jim's rival remains trapped inside his cab and dies. On September 30, 1955, the same year as he made *Rebel without a Cause*, James Dean hurtled to his death at the wheel of a Porsche.

"We say *gioventù bruciata* [the title given the film in Italy; the phrase means "burnt-out youth"] but it is truly a very dismissive attitude," wrote Fernanda Pivano in *America*. "Because if this image evokes James Dean and his legacy of misunderstood adolescence it has little to do with young people who have deliberately chosen to forego a facile security and isolated themselves in a separate society unshackled

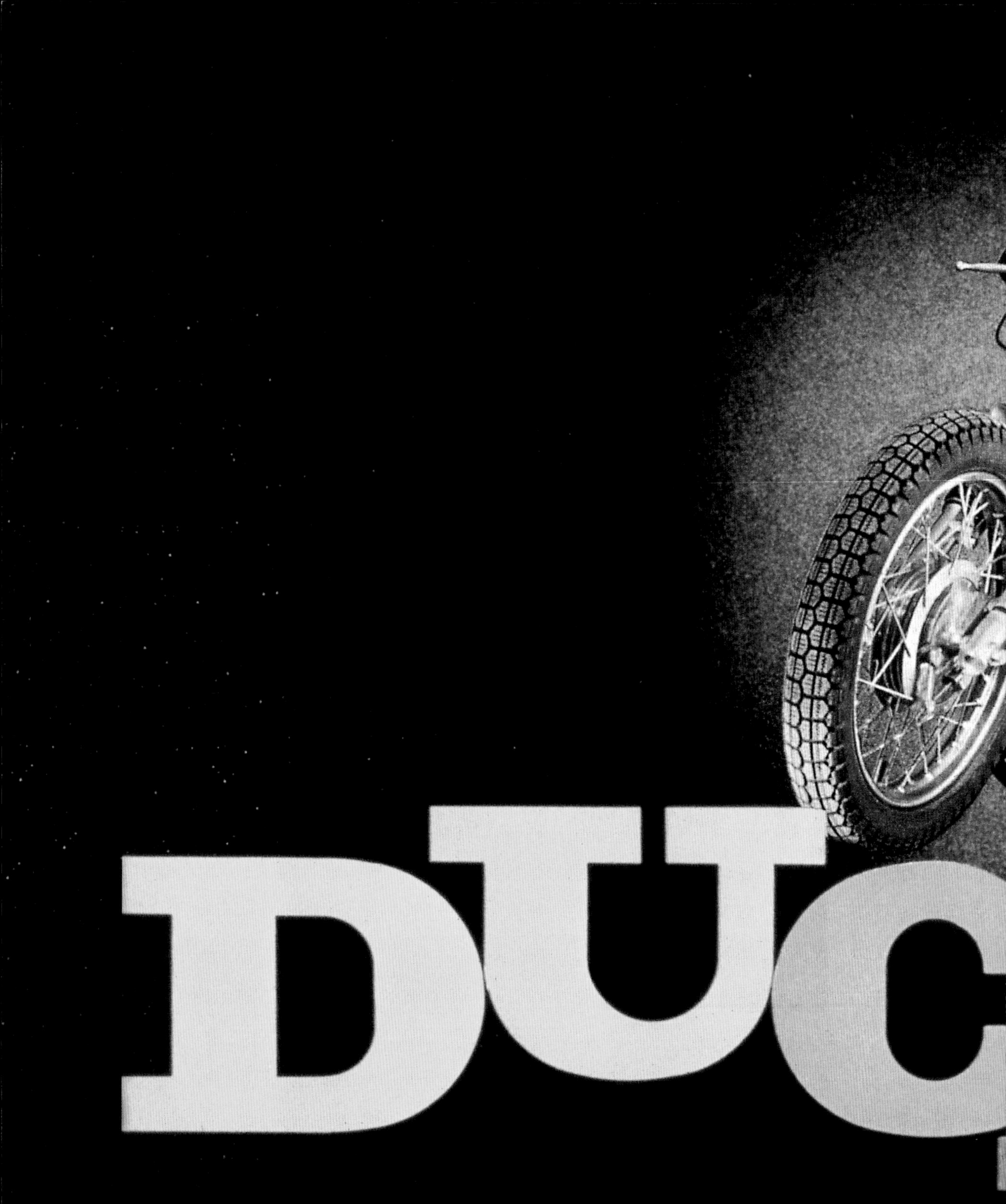
DUC

by current social norms. The beatniks' independence has often elicited comparisons, in moral terms, with juvenile delinquents and, in literary terms, with the lost generation. These are two extremely facile but rather arbitrary comparisons … In reality the beats reject the young delinquents as the most conformist of all. The young delinquent, in fact, stakes everything on the transitional values of the American myth: he covets success and celebrity, he is avid for wealth and power. He succumbs to ambitions and vanity worthy of the old bootleggers and is obsessed speed and the desire to appear fearless and reckless. The famous portrait of Marlon Brando in *The Wild One* is much more the portrait of a juvenile delinquent than a beatnik …"

Astride a motorbike, his bond with a group of nomadic bikers, Johnny (Marlon Brando) in Laszlo Benedek's *The Wild One* (1954) wears a black leather jacket, the emblem of his membership of the Black Rebels. They roar into a peaceful small town, where Johnny saves the life of Kitty (Mary Murphy), the sheriff's daughter. Kitty falls in love with him and her father clears Johnny of the murder of his rival Chino (Lee Marvin).

Observes Hunter S. Thompson, in *Hell's Angels*: "The truth is that *The Wild One*—despite an admittedly fictional treatment—was an inspired piece of film journalism. Instead of institutionalizing common knowledge, in the style of Time, it told a story that was only beginning to happen and which was inevitably influenced by the film.

It gave the outlaws a lasting romance-glazed image of themselves, a coherent reflection that only a few had been able to find in a mirror, and it quickly became the bike rider's answer to *The Sun also Rises*. The image is not valid, but its wide acceptance can hardly be blamed on the movie. *The Wild One* was careful to distinguish between 'good outlaws' and 'bad outlaws,' but the people who were most influenced chose to identify with Brando instead of Lee Marvin, whose role as the villain was more true to life than Brando's portrayal of the confused hero. They saw themselves as modern Robin Hoods … virile, inarticulate brutes whose good instincts got warped somewhere in the struggle for self-expression and who spent the rest of their violent lives seeking revenge on a world that had done them wrong when they were young and defenseless. … The concept of the 'motorcycle outlaw' was as uniquely American as jazz. Nothing like them had ever existed. In some ways they appeared to be a kind of half-bred anachronism, a human hangover from the era of the Wild West. Yet in other ways they were as new as television. There was absolutely no

"In the sixties and well beyond the Scrambler defined a style of life."
Marco Montemaggi

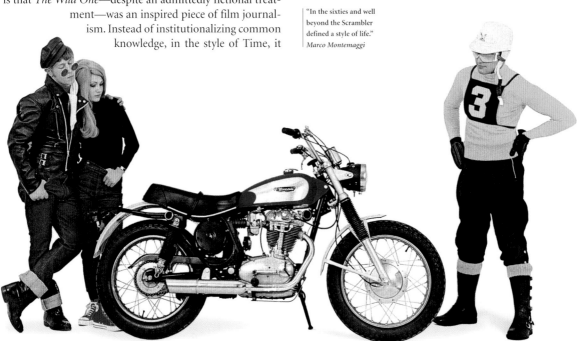

precedent, in the years after the Second World War, for large gangs of hoodlums on motorcycles, reveling in violence, worshipping mobility and thinking nothing of riding five hundred miles on a weekend. ... to whoop it up with other gangs of cyclists in some country hamlet entirely unprepared to handle even a dozen peaceful tourists."

It was also in 1954 that Alberto Sordi appeared as Nando Moriconi in Steno's *Un Americano a Roma*. The film is an irresistible portrait of a *borgataro*, a working class boy from Rome, who speaks Italian with an American accent, obsessively watches American movies and apes the behavior of the stars of the day. He tries to forsake macaroni for yogurt and jam, wine for a tumbler of milk, but the effort is beyond him. Every day he wishes he had been born in Kansas City, the America of his imagination. He dons an improbable uniform and drives along the Roman consular roads astride a high-powered motorcycle, impersonating an American cop on motorbike patrol. He flags down astonished motorists and indicates unlikely deviations that get them into serious trouble. The figure of Nando Moriconi, his uniform, the way he grips the handlebars, props the bike on its stand or jams on his sunglasses, his posture on the bike, are all the inventions of a great comic actor, while "Pulling over, halting, are disagreeable operations," say Prato and Trivero. "And the rider hates going someplace or seeing someone because, at his ease only on the seat of his bike, even when stopped, the motorbike still embodies for these young proletarians the wanderlust and craving for speed spread by the revolution in transport, together with a desire for the somewhere far away. ... The bike allows for no behavior other than riding, the mind cannot be distracted, the body is subordinated to the movement of the vehicle and has to mediate its impact on the environment. It is perhaps its dependence on the environment that has prevented the bike from being assimilated to bourgeois culture, since this culture—especially in its decadent phase—sees the experience of travel as a replica of home life, with its luxuries and comforts. The motorbike has no interior, it presents itself as form devoid of

content; the impact with the environment is not filtered by a cab that enables the individual to remain himself regardless of the landscape he is traversing ... If a motor-vehicle (container) evokes a reality alien to the subject (in terms of social class, lifestyle, convictions), a vehicle/gadget like the motorbike also has the function of being possessed, not just used, and in this sense it evokes its owner, his private world. It reinforces the personality while his personality acts on the vehicle and modifies it in his own image and likeness: high flared handlebars are made to ride in an erect position that reduces speed and road holding but improves the rider's abilities and increases the effect of the wind. The conventional motorcyclist does the opposite: he lowers the handlebar and pushes the footpegs back so his body stretches our and enhances airflow ..."

following pages
Dennis Hopper, who directed and starred in *Easy Rider*, said: "Basically I just swapped symbols: roads and motorbikes instead of prairies and horses."

While everywhere the *Ducatisti's* behavior corresponds to that of the conventional motorcyclist, in the United States, especially at that time, people rode with bust erect on their bikes, strong and flexible on every road, whether highway or dirt track.

In 1961 the 250cc version of the Scrambler fulfilled the dream of Ducati lovers across the Atlantic, thanks to its importer Joe Berliner; this was even before it was marketed in Europe, where it arrived later among the symbols of the American dream. "In the 1950s–'60s Joe Berliner was far and away the best of Ducati's customers," states Livio Lodi, "and so he had the power to influence the firm's policies. He encouraged the project of an all-purpose bike that would appeal to young people but also revive the youth of the not-so-young. Remember that in those years, in Europe and above all in Italy, the *utilitarie* like the new Fiat 500 penalized sales of motorbikes with medium-large engines. Berliner knew that in the States cars would never affect motorcycle sales, the two market segments were nurtured by completely different dreams…"

In the 1970s there was a recrudescence of the American myth of the frontier. Dennis Hopper visited Milan on December 7, 1998, the first day of the opera season, for the opening of his personal exhibition of photography at the Trussardi Foundation in Palazzo Marino alla Scala. In conversation with me, he said of *Easy Rider*, the film that did most to make his name: "Basically I just swapped symbols: roads and motorbikes instead of prairies and horses."

As Prato and Trivero note: "The motorcycle rather than the car guides that infinite odyssey on the road, underscoring a shift from the herd instinct to the headiness of independence. If the automobile, also an objective of transgressive uses, fully embodies the ambiguity of domestic life, the motorbike's intrinsic instability makes it an even better representative of decentered lifestyles. The road is an analogue of adolescence, which divides life into a before and after. The biker in the America of the dream was the lifelong adolescent, a full-time inhabitant of the road…"

Dennis Hopper, Billy in *Easy Rider* (1969), and Peter Fonda, Wyatt, called Captain America, traverse the States on their high-handlebar choppers. The film combines rebellion, music and drugs. The drugs, in turn, take on symbolic valences: cocaine is profit, marijuana sociability, LSD nightmare. Billy and Wyatt are in quest of a new frontier, though their adventure will not be that of the cowboy of tradition but of the Indian

my recording studio. I'd sell my house … but my motorbike—never!"

Perhaps the finest hymn to the Scrambler was not penned by a poet or songwriter: it is the story that Graziano Marzioni, from Tolentino in the province of Macerata, a lifelong adolescent, entrusted to his writer friend: "I'm not a motorcyclist and I know almost nothing about engines, but I do cherish one authentic passion, a passion for my Scrambler. In everyone's memory, emotions, places and feelings are held together by a few significant objects; for me the Scrambler is one of these. I dreamt of it as an adolescent, when I heard it go thundering through the town ridden by some proud kid. At the age of nineteen I quickly nabbed the opportunity to get one myself, when a

who goes to his tragic destiny: like their traveling companion George Hanson (an unforgettable Jack Nicholson), who is radically excluded even earlier. In its cinematic fiction, *Easy Rider* interprets and testifies to the tensions among young Americans at the time, while not long after the TV stereotype was given Fonzie's sugary smile. Lounging in his saddle, caressing the tank, the hero exclaims: "The chopper, hell no, you can't touch the chopper." And here Marco Montemaggi and Livio Lodi concur that the bike in the film, though camouflaged for the needs of the show, was probably a Ducati Scrambler, one of the many sold by the importer Joe Berliner in America. As Marco Montemaggi points out: "In the 1960s and long after the Scrambler defined a lifestyle, just as now, thirty years later, the Monster does …"

In 1970 Lucio Battisti sang *Il Tempo di Morire*: "Motocicletta / 10 H P / Tutta cromata / è tua se dici sì / Mi costa una vita / per niente la darei / Ma ho il cuore malato / e so, che guarirei". ("Motorcycle / 10 HP / All chrome metal / It's all yours if you say yes / But it costs me my life / I'd never give it away / But my heart is sick / and I know I'll get better that way.")

Lyrics by Mogol fail to name of the motorcycle. But in the *Ducati Yearbook* the singer/songwriter Lucio Dalla declares: "My Ducati Scrambler 250 is kept under glass, under lock and key, in a vacuum chamber, in

fellow draftee, during a long night's guard duty, confessed he had one in his brother's house, stowed away in an old barn. I snapped it up. It was only thirteen years younger than me, though it looked a lot older. It was full of ailments and bore the marks of a dangerous life, but it still retained intact that dignity that enchanted me as a boy. I nursed it all through the summer, seeking out the leading specialists in the area, those who had known, owned, or simply admired it. After long efforts its wounds were finally healed and its voice boomed out again, over-whelmingly, so that I too could thunder proud-ly through the town. The story might end here, banal and with a happy ending, but what most thrilled me in my relationship with the Scrambler were the moments, snapshots fixed in my memories: the oil curdled with dust and rust covering the faded orange and tarnished chrome; the bold sound of the engine as it recovers its pride with sudden, powerful detonations; the sweat streaming down my face, the fatigue and pushing in exchange for a moment's freedom; kick-starting it, the pain and the scars on my ankles; the innumerable rides, enriched by the warm, heartfelt embrace of my woman or the curious and worried looks of my children, and the hills of my land."

Henry Winkler, Fonzie in *Happy Days*. Marco Montemaggi and Livio Lodi agree that the bike, camouflaged for the needs of the show, was probably a Scrambler Ducati.

Lorenzo Cherubini, in art Jovanotti, wrote *La Musica della razza urbana*, the introduction to

1971, 750 GT
Designed by Taglioni,
the 750 GT was Ducati's
first approach to
producing a powerful
roadster.

Potere alla Parola: "Rap is a sound, a sound that changes but still a sound. Just as the blues are a sound quite apart from its harmonic scale, so rap, apart from its four-four time, is rap because it has the rap sound. There are many kinds of rap that miss the rap sound, they simply travesty it. The sound of rap is recognizable to those who live the context of rap, those who breathe its air, those who vibrate to it. For others rap is a piece, a song that has something they like, as happens with songs: out of many just one catches your fancy and you want to listen to it without thinking if it is this or that, if its sound has a story and what story. Rap is the sound of today; it is the sound for which these years will be remembered musically by the historians of 2500 BC. Any music born today has to come to terms with that sound, and will inevitably be influenced by it…"

So *La mia moto* is a sound of today: "…la puzza di benzina mi fa girar la testa/quando sto su di

following pages
The 750 GT made a strikingly explicit statement of its reassuring reserves of power.

lei è proprio la mia festa/mi guardo quando passo sui vetri dei negozi/mi accorgo che con lei mi sento proprio Fonzie." ("The gas fumes make me dizzy / When I'm out riding I have a lot of fun / I'm mirrored in the store windows / When I'm out riding I realize I feel like Fonzie.")

The Scrambler is a way of life, it has nothing to do with the untamed passion for racing that has always distinguished *Ducatisti* all over the world. "Unfortunately," observes Livio Lodi, "because of the frequency of fatal accidents, road races, continuing day and night and with the crowds lining the roads, gave way to protected circuits where the fearless viewers would soon be transformed into spectators, thronging the stands and fenced paddocks. At that point, the Ducati management decided to close down the racing team and the school for riders. They staked their future on the production of road bikes, since the marque was now in such demand all over the world. Consequently, in the years that followed, the firm no longer financed racing directly. There was the exemplary case of Mike Hailwood, a young English rider, the son of a magnate, who turned up at Borgo Panigale to race for Ducati. When he was told that team had pulled out of racing, without

more ado his father said he would personally finance the whole undertaking. So Fabio Taglioni got the chance to work on an engine with twin parallel cams produced in three different engine sizes: 150, 250 and 350cc. Hailwood Senior chose the 250cc machine for his son and he began to win on the English circuits, making a name for Ducati across the Channel. Taglioni used to joke that he was certainly a great rider but his long feet ruined the Ducati 250's good looks. Villa raced the 125 and Surtees the 350 …"

During the late sixties and early seventies Japanese bikes flooded all the markets and there was urgent need of a new strategy to hold back their big-engine production models. In 1971 Taglioni designed the 750 GT as Ducati's version of a powerful maxi-moto. The 750 GT was striking by its explicit formal declaration of reassuring power. The open double cradle frame clearly revealed the power unit, a two-cylinder four-stroke longitudinal V set at 90 degrees. The design of the telehydraulic front forks, swinging rear forks and adjustable hydraulic shock absorbers all heightened the sense of the machine's formidable power, set off by the design of the fuel tank ledged against the long two-seater saddle.

"Taglioni had the gift of rendering his ideas in terms of workshop practice, making them immediate and comprehensible, before setting them down on the drawing board," recalls Giuliano Peretti. "In the evenings he worked out the details, the fruit of those inspired insights that often flashed into his mind as he watched a part being turned on a lathe or correcting the way a workman managed a file. His commitment was that of a champion, tightly focused, aiming directly the result. Throughout his long season at Ducati he never spared himself. He would be at the factory at all hours, especially when assiduously putting the finishing touches to a project. The 750 GT was the first production model to mount disk brakes and a fiberglass-plastic tank, which was notable if you see the innovation in relation to the period. Not to mention the absolute modernity of the engine, with some wholly original features. For instance the L-shaped angle of the cylinders, a 90-degree V, designed to eliminate vibration, or the perfectly balanced cam and connecting rods. The 750 GT was a great bike, easy to steer and very safe."

"The 750 GT was the first
production model to mount
disk brakes and a fiberglass
tank, which was notable
if you see the innovation
in terms of the period.
Not to mention the absolute
modernity of the engine,
with some wholly original
features."
Giuliano Pedretti

"At precisely this moment
someone, somewhere,
is getting ready to ride."
Melissa Holbrook Pierson

At the 200 Miglia in Imola,
1972, the "fantastic ride"
by Paul Smart, number 16,
and Bruno Spaggiari,
number 9.
"That victory clinched
the firm's interest in racing:
from that day on it thought
almost exclusively in terms
of racing bikes derived from
production models."
Marco Masetti

In *Zen and the Art of Motorcycle Maintenance*, Robert M. Pirsig writes: "That's all the motorcycle is, a system of concepts worked out in steel. There's no part in it, no shape in it, that is not out of someone's mind … I've noticed that people who have never worked with steel have trouble seeing this—that the motorcycle is essentially a mental phenomenon. They associate metal with given shapes—pipes, rods, girders, tools, parts—all of them fixed and inviolable, and think of it as primarily physical. But a person who does machining or foundry work or forge work or welding sees 'steel' as having no shape at all. … Shapes, like this tappet, are what you *arrive* at, what you give to the steel. That's important to see. The steel? Hell, even the steel is out of someone's mind."

There is a curious parallel to be found here with Giuliano Pedretti's comments regarding the way Taglioni worked: "He knew how to translate his ideas into workshop practice, where it was finally possible to give a shape to the materials, to materialize the system of ideas that is called a motorcycle." "The true system, the real system, is our present construction of systematic thought itself, rationality itself," explains Pirsig, "and if a factory is torn down, but the rationality which produced it is left standing, then that rationality will simply produce another factory." This applies to the 750 GT, born for use on the roads: a year later Taglioni dismantled it and then turned it into one of the most celebrated racing bikes of all time.

"In 1972," writes Marco Masetti, "the 200 Mile formula, invented in the United States by the genius Checco Costa, reached Italy. As always, in record time (about a month later) Ducati had produced a set of eight bikes for Smart (signed up while he was racing in the States, through the good offices of his wife Maggie), Bruno Spaggiari, Ermanno Giuliano and Alan Dunscombe (another British rider chosen by the importer Vic

Rain or shine, bikers just can't stay home.

Camp). The racing bikes had the standard production frame and engine (they were taken off the assembly line), but the factory staff prepared them, as usual in a very short time (Farnè simply says 'working through the night') and with great passion. They concentrated on developing special rods, new camshafts and beautifully machined desmo systems … The bikes were honed to perfection, made lighter, care was lavished on them." So the step was taken from the 750 GT to the 750 Imola, after the city that hosted the 1972 200 Mile race of Ducati's victory in the maximoto class.

"Of Paul Smart and Bruno Spaggiari's fantastic ride," continues Masetti, "neck and neck right to the end, much has been written (and the two often gave discordant versions, especially about the amount of gas left in the tanks). But little has been said about how that race changed the destiny of the Italian firm, so that we are still experiencing its aftermath. That victory clinched the firm's interest in racing: from that day on it thought almost exclusively in terms of racing bikes derived from production models."

Unlike the 750 GT, the Imola had a limited fairing which sheathed the telescopic hydraulic front forks and wrapped

around the flanks, partly concealing the engine. In front the fairing rose to shape the Plexiglas cockpit, which rose above the handlebars and was raked back toward the fuel tank with its distinctive transparent strip for checking the fuel level.

"The appeal of the 750 GT," explains Giuliano Pedretti, "was definitely heightened by the 750 Imola's stunning victories. Thanks to the triumphs of this derivative of the production model, the Ducati 750 began to win a market niche that was no longer identified only with the Scrambler: it was now associated with big-engine bikes capable of handling the competition from Yamaha, Suzuki and Kawasaki. While other motorcycle makers designed and built special bikes for racing, quite different from the production models, Ducati was capable of designing a series model that also won races. This is a fact that increased and strengthened the confidence of the *Ducatisti* all over the world."

Twenty-five years earlier the mass-produced Cucciolo had gotten a similar boost from the performance of its racing derivatives. If the Imola was derived from the 750 GT, the design evolved further into models with even bigger engines. After his debut on a Ducati 250cc, Mike Hailwood rode a 900SS to victory in the Tourist Trophy on the Isle of Man and with it Ducati's first world championship.

"The story," continues Masetti, "almost the legend, of the 1978 world title won by Mike Hailwood on the Isle of Man riding a Ducati 900SS truly deserves to be fully understood. In 1977 the British rider had practically closed his career with a total of nine world motorbike titles and one Formula 2 car-racing championship. After an appalling accident in 1974 when driving for McLaren in Germany, Mike went to live with his wife in New Zealand: at most he would ride in minor races to keep up his old passion. At Silverstone in

In 1978 the 900SS enabled Mike Hailwood to win the Tourist Trophy on the Isle of Man and with it Ducati's first world championship. (He had made his debut on a Ducati 250cc.)

1977 he met Steve Wynne, concessionaire, former racing driver and race mechanic, the owner of Sport Motor Cycles Ltd in Manchester."
Jokingly the veteran British rider expressed a desire to race in the following year's T.T. Wynne took him at his word, signed him up on the spot, then ordered three of a batch of twenty 900s prepared for racing in endurance trials. The bikes had a molybdenum chrome frame made by Daspa and a sand-cast timing case which was reinforced and tapered at one end. Marco Montemaggi adds details that heighten the legend of that victory on the Isle of Man.
"This was a difficult, dangerous urban course—stiff climbs to the top of sharp ridges were followed by hurtling descents leading into tight bends. Mike was a specialist in this kind of racing but he had long abandoned motorbikes for Formula 2 cars. When Wynne took the three Ducati 900SS, he also secured the help of two outstanding technicians—Franco Farnè and Giuliano Pedretti. Note that the 900SS was a big bike, not designed for racing, derived from the production model. When he threw the machine into a curve Mike's long feet would rub against the asphalt so he wore the leather off his boots. By the end of a race his feet were always bleeding but Hailwood never even noticed."
An emblematic figure, a myth within the Ducati myth, Mike Hailwood raced with the 250 when the Borgo Panigale firm had given up designing special racing machines: it just used derivatives of its production models for the purpose. And

1980, Pantah
The beautiful architecture
of the engine anchored
at three points to the
tubular-steel trestle frame,
the reduced lateral fairing
that projects to form
the transparent cockpit
and gives free play to the
telescopic-hydraulic forks
with their advanced inner
pivots.

here it is just as well to stress once more that the intention of no longer making a clear separation between the two projects, production and racing, won Ducati the fame of being a house that could win on both fronts: road bikes and racers. Mike Hailwood remained an outstanding witness to Ducati's evolutionary arc.

"All things considered there exist only two kinds of men in the world: those that stay at home and those that do not," observed Rudyard Kipling. For enterprise and daring Hailwood definitely belonged to the second group, just like the motorcyclist to whom Melissa Holbrook Pierson applies this observation.

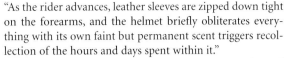

"At precisely this moment someone, somewhere, is getting ready to ride. The motorcycle stands in the cool, dark garage, its air expectant with gas and grease. The rider approaches from outside; the door opens with a whir and a bang. The light goes on. A flame, everlasting, seems to rise on a piece of chrome.

"As the rider advances, leather sleeves are zipped down tight on the forearms, and the helmet briefly obliterates everything with its own faint but permanent scent triggers recollection of the hours and days spent within it."

The vague persistent smell has the power to evoke and define the shape of past episodes.

"Soft leather gloves with studded palms, insurance against the reflex of a falling body to put its hands out in midair, go on last.

"The key is slipped into the ignition at the top of the steering head. Then the rider swings a leg over the seat and sits but keeps the weight on the balls of his feet. With a push from the thighs the rider rocks the bike forward just once, again, picking up momentum until it starts to fall forward and down from the centerstand. At this moment the rider pulls a lever with the first finger of the right hand, and the brake pads close like a vice on the front wheel's iron rotor. At the almost instantaneous release of the brake the bike rises slightly from the forks, which had telescoped under the heft. Now the 450 pounds of metal, fluid, and plastic rests in tenuous balance between the rider's legs; if it started to lean too much to one side, the weight that had lain low in a state of grace would suddenly assert itself in a manic bid to meet the concrete with a crash. Inherently unstable at a standstill, the bike is waiting for the human help to become its true self. Out there running, it can seem as solid as stone.

"The key turns; the idiot lights glow. The green is for neutral gear, the red for the battery, another red for oil pressure. The starter button on the right handlebar, pressed, begins a whirring below. A simultaneous twist of the right grip pulls the throttle cables and the engine bleats, then gulps, then roars. A contained fire has been lit within inches of the rider's knees. As the plugs in the two cylinders, posed in a 90-degree V, take their inestimably quick turns in sparking a volatile cocktail of fuel and compressed oxygen, the expanding gases forcing back the pistons, the machine vibrates subtly from side to side."

Truly fine this sequence: the breath held until the completion of starting, a precise ritual that breathes life into the stationary bike.

"The two V cylinders, set at an angle of 90 degrees, say a lot about the identity of the bike," notes Livio Lodi, "though Pierson doesn't mention it."

The Italian Guzzi and Ducati are numbered among the perfect vehicles: "A flip of the headlight switch on the handlebar throws the garage walls to either side into theatrical relief. (The rider knows to run through all the lights—turn signals, taillight, brake lights tripped by hand and foot—to make sure they work, but is sometimes guilty of neglecting this step.) The rider pulls in the left-hand lever, then presses down with the left foot. There's a solid chunk as first gear engages.

"In the neat dance that accomplishes many operations on a motorcycle—one movement to countered by another from, an equilibrium of give and take—the squeezed clutch lever is slowly let out while the other hand turns the throttle grip down. The bike moves out into a brighter world where the sun startles the rider's eyes for a moment and washes everything in a continual pour.

"Out in the early-morning street there is little traffic, for which the rider sends up thanks: on a bike, cars are irksome, their slow-motion ways infuriating. Pulling out of the drive, the rider shifts into second, this time with the boot toes under the lever to push it up. The small jolt of increased speed from the rear wheel is experienced in the seat, just as in the elastic pause when a horse gathers strength in its haunches before springing into a canter from a trot.

"To warm up the tires, the rider shifts so slightly in the seat it is hardly noticeable except to the bike, which dips left. Then quickly right again, then left, then right, until the machine is drawing a sinuous S down the road. They could dance like this all day, partnered closely and each anticipating the next step so surely it is not at all clear who is who."

One sunny morning, like a new pedagogic Cheiron, the centaur-biker reawakens and regains familiarity with the whole mechanism of his body, interprets it, explains it, articulates its responses, moves alone amid different presences, until the whole population of centaurs finally awakens and looks out on the landscape. "As they reach the exurban limits and turn onto a narrow road that ascends among trees and infrequent stone houses set back in the shadows, other riders are accelerating up highway ramps; riding gingerly in first gear between two lanes of traffic jammed on a city bridge; hitting the dirt front-wheel-first after being launched from the top of a hillock in a field; trying to pass a motor home making its all-too-gradual way into a national park; feeling a charge move from stomach to chest as the bike straightens up from the deepest lean it's yet entered ..."

The population of centaurs, in the words of Melissa Holbrook Pierson, reawakens to the experience of play, of movement, of speed, of flight from all forms of resignation and constraint. This is in total contrast with the behavior of motorists, who substitute the cab of the saloon car for their living room at home. Rain or shine, bikers just can't stay home.

Especially when the bike is the fastest, the most powerful in the world, like the Ducati Pantah 500 in 1980. "To those who love motorcycles deeply, there is usually one aspect of the machine that broadcasts its allure in advance of all others. It may be the visual arrangement of parts, their rake and line and organization that come together in a design that seems to freeze speed. ... For me, it is their sound that makes the heart race. The exhaust notes of certain bikes functions like an aria, the relentlessly plaintive song that arrives at the vulnerable moment in the opera to wring the emotions dry. ... The sounds of Italian engines, especially those of Moto Guzzis and Ducatis, are to me so supremely sensuous that I can only merely appreciate—albeit appreciate well—the tone of other bikes."

The comparison is far from casual, because the opera-lover, though moved by the whole opera repertoire, is truly exalted only by that music, by those voices that more than any other arouse incommensurable emotions. The voice of the Pantah 500 has a full, velvety, seductive timbre; the middle range is full-bodied, rising in pitch to clear, precise high notes that pierce your bones. As an object the Pantah is also a vector of further emotions: the beautiful architecture of the engine anchored at three points to the tubular-steel trestle frame; the reduced lateral fairing that projects to form the transparent cockpit and gives free play to the telescopic-hydraulic forks with their advanced inner pivots. Becoming even more rarefied at the back, the fairing is cut away at the tail behind the elongated saddle, leaving the swinging forks conspicuously looking naked with their adjustable hydraulic shock absorbers.

"The season of the 750 GT and its racing derivatives certainly helped strengthen Ducati's credibility internationally," observes Livio Lodi. "But the bikes that had won at Imola and on the Isle of Man, and were now thundering along the roads of half the world, still belonged to the first evolutionary arc of the company, though they were its finest expression. The transition from bevel gears to belt drive was a fundamental stage in Ducati's evolution in design and production, and the Pantah was the key model in this development."

Luigi Mengoli, a key figure at Ducati, recalls, "Fabio Taglioni commissioned me in 1978 to work on the actual development of the design and my study led to the conception of

Ducati's current engines. In fact, if the 750 evolved the tried and tested one-cylinder engine into a two-cylinder engine with bevel gear drive, the Pantah had a quite different drive system and was therefore to all effects a new two-cylinder engine. The Pantah was half-way between the first-generation engines and those that lay in the future, because it began a new season in design and production at Ducati. Its esthetic definition was Franco Bilancioni's greatest achievement."

So the Pantah marked a breakthrough, renewed the basic principles of engine design, and opened up new market horizons for the firm of Borgo Panigale. It soon succeeded in mass-producing some of the world's fastest and most beautiful bikes.

"Ducati was winning races for derivatives of production bikes," observes Franco Bilancioni, "so I tried to foreground the machine's racing qualities. And since the engine embodied this quality, in its completely new conception, I decided to leave it open and actually emphasize its massive proportions, which were striking. A steel trestle frame was best suited to this purpose. And the big fuel tank, surmounting the powerful architecture of the power assembly, helped to define a very effective compact configuration."

So the Pantah was born to thrill: at Ducati design has always meant thrills. "Even the inept-

ness of the executives who followed each other in running the firm as long as it was state-owned failed to denature Ducati design," observes Marco Montemaggi. "Officially racing was put on hold during these long troubled years, until finally, in 1983, Romano Prodi, president of the IRI (state holding company), decided to cede Ducati to the Castiglione brothers who owned the Cagiva firm in Varese. But unofficially the Ducati bikes continued to express their natural bent in the workshops of racing mechanics. One for all: NCR, based on the western edge of Bologna."

NCR was a small firm founded by two partners who possessed real mechanical genius: Rino Caracchi and Giorgio Nepoti. (When Rizzi left the R of the acronym was made to stand for "racing".) "Supported by Farnè, Pedretti, Recchia, Cavazzi and also *Ingegnere* Taglioni, they made some wonderful bikes … But what was NCR?" asks Marco Masetti. "A workshop that prepared racing bikes or a full-scale racing outfit? The answer is complex and I prefer not to respond directly. NCR was a great school of biking, but also something more: it was the embodiment of a biking philosophy that held that everything can be improved, everything can be made lighter. Because one single horse-power is made up of many fractions, the way a kilo is made up of a thousand grams. Because even the most commonplace of screws can function better and be unscrewed quicker, perhaps at a vital moment in a race, if its function has been rationalized.

There were no computers at NCR (they didn't exist then) but those men carried around whole data banks in their heads. Even today, if you ask one of them for an opinion about a bike or something that happened they still

remember everything, even a single touch of a file."

Melissa Holbrook Pierson writes: "The urge to compete on motorcycles appeared at about the same time as the conveyance was born. This is the same urge that has children pedaling like mad against their playmates within a day of receiving training wheels. The earliest race including motorcycles I can find mention of took place between Paris and Rouen; in 1894, perhaps it was an open-class free-for-all among automobiles, boneshakers, and gas-powered tricycles. In the next year America saw the first formal race with motorcycles entered—Chicago to Waukegan (although the first accredited race in the United States, from Boston to New York, had to wait until 1901 and the creation of an accrediting body).

"In 1897 in Britain there was a match between a motorcycle and a bicycle, and *Horseless Vehicle Journal* opined that although the bicycle won the twenty-seven-mile race by three hundred yards, it would not be long before motors would reign over pedals."

Its technology gradually evolving, the bicycle pushed the limits of natural manpower, the engine the potential of artificial power, the machine, the motorbike.

"Speed, in its pure form, was the endlessly beckoning the challenger from the beginning, and the heights achieved so early became all the more incredible when you recognize that the more powerful the engine, the more critical the chassis. Since the adequacy of the latter frequently lags considerably behind the power of the former, the potential for disaster rises proportionately to the discrepancy. Aviation pioneer and avid motorcyclist Glenn Curtiss installed in a bike chassis a Curtiss transverse V-8 with shaft drive; its unofficial time was 136.3 mph at Ormond Beach—in 1907. In 1920, a 1114cc Indian V-Twin registered 115.79 mph at Daytona Beach, and by 1937 the world speed record was 170.5 mph, set by Piero Taruffi on a Gilera. The mark lasted less than a month, retaken by the German Ernst Henne on a BMW at 173.5 mph. Henne was the holder, however briefly, of seventy-six world records."

The racing project increasingly pushed for greater power plus greater safety through more reliable running gear.

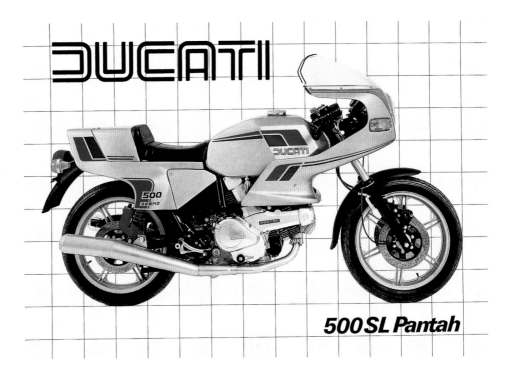

DUCATI

500 SL Pantah

"The history of racing can in fact be broken into blocks of the years and sometimes decades in which certain countries' engines took more trophies than any others: the French, British and Americans tossed the wins back and forth in the century's first couple of decades; in the 1930s England's Norton machine seemed invincible; the Italians fought back hard and often successfully in the latter part of that decade, while right before the Second World War, BMW looked poised to steal the lead. The end of the fifties marked the end of the golden age of British bikes, by which time Italy had become a star once more, notably with Guzzi and Gilera. At the beginning of the sixties the products of the manufacturer MV (Meccanica Verghera) Agusta, the rich child of Count Domenico Agusta, blasted to win after win all over the

Continent: they won world championships in 1958, 1959 and 1960 in the 500cc, 350cc and 250cc classes. (The only one they didn't win, in fact, was the sidecar competition, which had always belonged to BMW.) The decades of Japanese supremacy began in 1961 …"

Then followed a long period characterized by the stunning victories of the big Japanese bikes, while motorcycle-makers world-wide struggled to stem the tide. Among them was Ducati and the by now legendary Fabio Taglioni. An outstanding example was the 750 GT in 1971. The great Romagnolo designer was due to retire into private life in 1983, when Ducati finally passed from state ownership into the hands of the Castiglioni brothers. This was forty years after his first challenge, the design of the 100cc Gran Sport, which became a legend under the name of Marianna. Taglioni passed on the torch to Massimo Bordi, but continued working as a consultant for Ducati up to 1992.

"It seemed their sovereignty would have no end," concludes Melissa Pierson, "and then came the beginning of the nineties, when the Italian firm of Ducati reappeared on the world scene with its startlingly powerful red superbikes."

Norina Taglioni describes the forty years of her husband's passionate loyalty to the firm at Borgo Panigale. "He did not just design motorcycles, he oversaw their development in the factory and even when they were racing, especially at the trials, when the bikes' potential and the riders' skills were being tested, he would thrash out ways to optimize both in front of a scale drawing of the circuit. He would explain to the rider the correspondence between the gears he was using and the particular design of the track and at the same time suggest choices in when to shift up or down. 'But you're capable of going faster at this precise point, in this place here,' when he understood that the machine's power had to correspond to the man's daring. My husband had known Tazio Nuvolari when the Mantuan was already driving racing cars after a spectacular season on bikes. Nuvolari later introduced Fabio to Enzo Ferrari, who tried all his wiles to get him away from motorbikes and entice him to Maranello. Though he was proud of Ferrari's confidence, Fabio believed that no single engineer could design a racing car and the idea of having to depend on others had no appeal for him. 'And then, if you find I'm not up to the job, just think how much of your money I'll have wasted.' Drake would gaze at him thoughtfully: 'I'm quite confident you can do it.' Fabio always resisted these offers. But when they were working on the Dino, Ferrari came to see us. He was sad and asked Fabio to help him complete the project in memory of his son, who had died young. Then Fabio had no hesitation and worked willingly on the project. One day, while the 750s were doing trials, my husband saw Ferrari at the Modena circuit and waved hello. At once Milvio and Spairani from Ducati, with him at the time, asked for an introduction to Drake (Ferrari's nickname), who at once invited all three to Maranello, telling Fabio to show them over the racing division. 'You know more than me about my company, and you still won't come and work for us.' Ferrari gave Fabio Taglioni the entrée to the racing division but my husband took advantage of it only in exceptional cases, when for example the shortsightedness of Ducati's management was stinting the supply of costly materials. At

"The urge to compete on motorcycles appeared at about the same time as the conveyance was born."
Melissa Holbrook Pierson

A truly fantastic bike that at once won the hearts of many fans and was the starting point of Ducati's history in the busy decade that began at the end of the 1970s.
Luigi Bianchi, Marco Masetti

Vesti i colori della tua
Wear the colours of your

these times Fabio used to phone Drake and send Mario Recchia over to Maranello. He would soon be back with the wherewithal to carry on experiments. Ferrari went so far as to offer Fabio the profits from a service and maintenance center he wanted to set up for private Ferrari customers, housed in a building in Modena on the western Via Emilia. 'You've never been paid what you're worth and you've got no nose for business, but at least you'll be secure and you can come to Maranello and design engines.' It was a really tempting offer and it wasn't the only one. At that time Maserati was also making overtures. Now I remember, one day Fabio decided to go to Modena to look into this offer and just as he was going through Borgo Panigale the driver of a car going the other way fell asleep at the wheel and crashed head-on into him. He ended up in hospital with eleven stitches in his face and every part of his body aching. When he finally came home he said: 'Norina, it was a sign. It means I mustn't move from Ducati.' And so it was, even though Honda and later Kawasaki kept holding out increasingly tempting baits. Enamored of Ducati, Fabio could never bring himself to betray it. A Romagnolo always needs good reasons to change his job. Fabio had only ever done so once, when Mondial's bikes won the championship and they never invited him to the party to celebrate."

An affectionate evocation of an adventure lived together in the name of an uncompromising passion, total commitment, a faith never betrayed.

"Taglioni or Mengoli … perhaps they don't even know the reason for that name: Pantah. And yet the Pantah project has become the goal of Ducati engines past and present," reflects Marco Montemaggi. "The name is inspired by the animal form, or rather the behavior typical of the noble cat, compared to the engine's architecture. A panther crouching to spring …"

Luigi Bianchi and Marco Masetti write: "A truly fantastic bike, it immediately won the heart of many fans and was the starting point of Ducati's history in the busy decade that began at the end of the 1970s. The new two-cylinder engine with a single cam desmodromic drive was a truly modern project. … The

500SL Pantah

1987, 851
The 851 established Ducati
in that market niche where
the interests are wholly
sporting.

Pantah convinced the testers of the period: 'almost 50 HP delivered to the wheels and 200 kmh. This was the outstanding performance revealed by our tests. The new two-cylinder engine boasted powerful torque, great stability and sparing fuel consumption. It was also distinguished by its exclusive technical features. But there were still a number of details to be ironed out.' It was the first two-cylinder Ducati with silent mechanicals (thanks to the belt drive that replaced the bevel gears). There were also some glitches … the clutch, for example, tended to swell under strain making it difficult to find neutral, while the hard seat and rigid suspension made for a rather uncomfortable ride. The fuel cap tended to leak … but it was easy to forgive these faults. With that engine Ducati raced (and won) in speed trials and in off-road races. The belt-driven engine ensured the success of dozens of different bikes …" Two can be taken as representative of all of them: the TT2 600cc and the TT1 750cc. Marco Masetti recounts their epic: "In 1982 the TT2 won the Italian title with Walter Cussigh, who dominated all the races, while Tony Rutter won the world title for the second year in a row … In 1983 Rutter was world champion for the second time; among other things, on the Isle of Man on the TT2 Tony took first place and Graeme McGregor second, while Walter Cussigh again won the Italian title. In 1983 Rutter was the winner. In Italy the title went to Fabio Barchitta on a 600 Ducati, while the newborn TT1 entrusted to Walter Villa won immediately … The TT1 differed in some details from the 600: the forks were strengthened with a truss, while

The 851's design was defined by the objective that Massimo Bordi set himself to achieve, a racing bike.

the wheels were equipped with pull-off wheels for use in endurance trials. While on the subject of the trials, it is worth mention that the TT1 raced at Le Mans in 1984 and came in fourth with the French riders Guichon, Vuillemin and Granie, fourth in the Austrian Thousand Kilometers, third in the 24 Hours of Liège, and fourth at the Six Hour Race of Mugello."

These achievements earned the Pantah 500 series a name for reliability, propelling it into the international market and distinguishing it among sport bikes for long-distance riding.

"The road, constantly turning, continually offers up the possibility of something unexpected around the bend—gravel in a tumult across the road, a car drifting over the yellow line, a dog maddened by the din from the pipes. The rider processes data from the road and its environs with a certain detachment, translating them nearly as quickly into physical response: eat or be eaten. There is no room in the brain for idle thought (except on the highway, when idle thoughts appear and float and reconfigure in endless array), and a biker can go for miles and miles without waking up to any sudden realization, including the one that nothing at all has been thought for miles and miles. The faster you ride, the more closed the circuit becomes, deleting everything but this second and the next, which are hurriedly merging. Having no past to regret and no future to await, the rider feels free. Looked at from this tight world, the other one with its gore and stickiness seems well polished and contained at last.

"This peculiar physiological effect, common to all high-concentration pursuits, may be why one finds among motorcyclists a large number of people who always feel as if there were a fire lit under them when they are sitting still. When they're out riding, the wind disperses the flame so they don't feel the terrible heat …

"Every rider of a motorcycle lives with a little of the same denial, which is after all healthy and spares us from living in a world made entirely of dread. It is also the price of admission to a day like this. If the rider wants, the throttle can be cracked open so suddenly the handlebars yank the arms, threatening to run away with that paltry creature on back now reduced to hanging on and enjoying the ride.

"The roar left to ring under the trees as the machine passes is like the laser arc of red drawn by a taillight in a long-exposure photograph at night. It is the ghost remnant of how the bike cleaved the air, and what the rider felt as gravity battled flight against the rider's body. The curves play games with the rider, and the rider is lost in the concentration it takes to match wits with an impressive opponent. How fast to enter this turn? The fact that you can be sadly mistaken is what gives the right choice its sweet taste …

"As the road leaves home farther and farther behind, it makes its own friendly advances to keep the rider happy: See, this is where you stopped your bike once and ate an apple from the tank bag and took off your boots to feel the damp grass beneath your socks; this is the place your beloved bought you a handful of fireballs when you stopped for gas. And there is always the danger that the unexpected around the bend may turn out not to be a danger to avoid, but a sight or smell that appears suddenly like a check in the mail."

Melissa Holbrook Pierson captures the experience of traveling by motorcycle, "as the road leaves home farther and farther behind." Traveling in any other vehicle, especially a car, brings the journey much closer to the significance of Jules Verne's imaginary journeys, as expounded by Roland Barthes (1915–1980) in *Myths of Today*: "In Verne the journey corresponds to an exploration of closure; and the accord between Verne and childhood stems not from a banal mystique of adventure but, on the contrary, from a shared relish for the finite which is expressed in the childish passion for huts and tents: closing oneself, installing oneself, inside something: that is the existential dream of Verne's childhood. The archetype of this dream is an almost perfect novel, *The Mysterious Island*, in which the man-child reinvents the world, fills it, isolates it, shuts himself up in it, and crowns this encyclopedic effort with the bourgeois attitude of appropriation: slippers, pipe, and the chimney hearth, while outside the tempest, meaning the infinite, rages in vain."

The inside of an automobile is increasingly crammed with simple and complex technological equipment, meant to ensure the comfort and safety of the person inside it, the equivalent of home to car. "Verne," Barthes continues, "did not seek in the least to enlarge the world by the Romantic paths of escapism or the mystical planes of the infinite: unceasingly he sought to contract it, to populate it, to reduce it to a known and enclosed space, which man can then inhabit comfortably: the world can draw everything out of itself; in order to exist, all it needs is man…"

Barthes notes that the continual gesture of reclusion leads man, in Verne's imagination, to resemble the mythical

Antaeus, son of Poseidon and Gaia. He would lie in wait for travelers near Ustica, where he lived, wrestle with them, vanquish them and adorn the temple dedicated to his father with their spoils. Antaeus was invulnerable, but only as long as he was touching his Mother Earth. Hercules, who encountered Antaeus, was able to vanquish him by heaving him onto his powerful shoulders and there crushing the life out of his body.

"Verne had a mania for fullness: with unflagging energy he set out to circumscribe the world and furnish it, filling it as full as an egg. His movement was exactly that of an eighteenth-century *Encyclopédiste* or Dutch painter: the world is finite, the world is crammed with materials that can be numbered and are contiguous. All an artist can do is to compile catalogues, draw up inventories, rummage in odd corners, and then set out human creations and instruments in serried ranks."

This is an interesting foreshadowing of the automobile, into whose cab it is possible to implode the whole world, so precluding adventure from travel.

Barthes concludes: "Through this world, triumphantly devoured by Verne's hero, often some desperado wanders, a prey to remorse and melancholy, the vestige of a faded Romantic age, heightening by contrast the health of the true masters of the world, exclusively concerned to adapt themselves successfully to situations whose complexity, not in the

least metaphysical, is due merely to some piquant caprice of geography."

The motorcycle does not implode anything at all; it is neither interior, temple nor catalogue. It is play, in the free play of one who rides it in wind, rain, cold, and the chill air; one who is aware of the landscape and shares in the adventure that becomes memory or an emotional response to the revelation of the marvelous around a bend. Unlike the automobile, the motorcycle is truly a vestige of a bygone Romantic age, it induces you to seize the occasion, and so casts its spell over all those who in their inner selves know nothing can take its place. In 1987, for Ducati fans the world over, emotion took the shape of the 851 model.

"The conception of the 851 went back a year earlier and was an integrated project," explains Massimo Bordi, "aimed at a precise objective: the creation of a racing bike. So its production version, a road bike, was intended for entry in superbike races for derivatives. The 851's engine had four desmo valves per cylinder and overhead cams driven by a cogged belt. It was water cooled, with electronic fuel injection and a very high travel/bore ratio. The chassis was based on a tubular trestle frame with progressive rear suspension and integral fairing forming a single surface. There were two air intakes to enable the engine to breathe more freely, one to cool the radiator, and two vents to dispose of the hot air. In addition it achieved the very highest coefficient of penetration. The road version naturally mounted turn lights as well.

Massimo Bordi graduated from Bologna University in Mechanical Engineering in 1975. He presented a thesis on the design of the big end with a four-valve desmo drive system. He joined Ducati in 1978. Eight years later his flair for innovation appeared to great advantage in the integral project for the 851 that made its debut at Bol d'Or and a year later snatched victory at Daytona. "The first series (the 200 production bikes necessary for certification) ended up in the hands of collectors and riders," write Luigi Bianchi and Marco Masetti. "Then the 851 was fielded in the newly born World Superbike Trophy. It ranked fifth at the end of the season, with victories by Lucchinelli at Zeltweg and Donington, despite the fact that the racing budget had been pared to the bone. Finally it was delivered to the concessionaires. The twin-cylinder 851 boosted Ducati's image worldwide and in Japan at once became a cult object." Its success was highly significant at a time when the maximoto market was still dominated by the Japanese.

"The road Superbike version," continue Bianchi and Masetti, "excited the test drivers, who had never expected such a powerful and generous engine. The road bike had problems, especially with the forecarriage. The glitches were eliminated from the SBK, which mounted 17-inch wheels instead of 16, but the surprising feature was the discovery that a twin-cylinder could actually outperform four-cylinder engines. And this was just the beginning. Year after year the bike was honed till it was right at the top of the four-stroke class. Many came to realize that Ducati was not just a synonym of sporting tradi-

"The Italian tricolor on the fairing was changed to Ducati red, making it the company's standard-bearer. The engine size rose to 888cc, and it became the bike to beat in all international competitions."
Marco Montemaggi

The tail set high made the bike more aerodynamic and heightened the profile of the power assembly jutting out at the back, like a claw gripping the rear wheel.

tion but also a laboratory of advanced technology." So the 851 was a completely new approach to motorcycle design, and this was not just true at Ducati.

"The first true four-valve bike," notes Marco Montemaggi, "radically altered the approach to designing engines, even among rival manufacturers. The first model sported the Italian colors (red, white and green) on the fairing, then the livery was changed to Ducati's red, making it the company's standard-bearer. The engine size was raised to 888cc, and it became the champion to beat in all international competitions."

The 851's design was defined by the objective that Massimo

in Ducati that went all the way back to 1961, when the Elite, a direct descendant of the mythical Marianna and the models that developed its design principles, was joined by the Scrambler, a true all-rounder. Just thirty years after the Scrambler made its debut on the American market, where it was a dazzling success before bouncing back and bringing the American dream to the Old World, in 1993 the Monster was born. But while Ducati owed the Scrambler to the insistence of Joe Berliner, the firm's American importer, the Monster was the fruit of the intuition of Miguel Galluzzi, one of the world's best-known designers." He agreed to meet me and I visited him at his workplace set amid the shady

Tubular trestle frame, progressive rear suspension and integral fairing forming a single surface. Two air intakes to enable the engine to breathe freely, one to cool the radiator, and two vents to dispose of the hot air.

Bordi set himself to achieve, a racing bike, and shared by his assistant Luigi Mengoli, who helped develop the project. The integral fairing was marked half-way up diagonally on both flanks by the outcropping of the upper tubes of the wrap-around trestle frame. The massive tank dominated its summit and was slotted round the handlebars surmounted by the cockpit. The tail was set high to make the bike more aerodynamic and heighten the profile of the power assembly which jutted out at the back, like a claw gripping the rear wheel. The shape of the fairing and the general riding setup for the first time enabled the rider lying over on bends to skim the track with his knee. And here the 851 offered Ducati buffs the chance to imitate the masterly riding on the world's race circuits. With the 851, Ducati improved its position in the market niche for exclusively high-performance bikes.

"Oddly enough" notes Livio Lodi, "just when the Ducati market seemed identified with the superb racing quality of its bikes and its complete mastery of advanced technologies had secured maximum reliability, a phenomenon emerged

hills of the Varese area one hot day in late July. Looming up in the doorway, he smilingly invited me in. Then he began to tell me his story.

"I was born in Argentina and then moved to the States to study mechanical engineering. I heard that in California there was a school of industrial design so I gave up engineering and enrolled at the Central College of Design in Pasadena. Sponsored by the automobile industry, in reality the school was oriented exclusively toward automobile design. I completed the course but my heart was set upon designing motorcycles. I come from a racing family and ever since I was a kid I had a craze for bikes. My first job was with Opel in Germany. I stayed there two years. I was also in contact with Honda Europe, which is based near Frankfurt. The directors were thinking of setting up a Design Center in Milan, which they did in late 1988. I worked there a short time, unable to reconcile my Latin outlook with their Japanese approach to things. In the meantime I was offered a consultancy at Cagiva. At Honda I was only allowed to design fully faired bikes and I was terribly frustrated by this.

SUPERBIKE
DESMOQUATTRO
888

The fairing, essential in competitions to achieve the best coefficient of penetration, is not essential in everyday biking for fun, for the pleasure of a trip to the coast, out to the countryside, or for weaving through heavy traffic in town. I kept thinking about this. What's more, I remembered my friends in California complaining about the cost of the original spares of sections of fairing for their bikes that had got damaged in bumps or falls. Often the total was over a third of the cost of the bike itself. I was aching to design a completely bare bike, I was convinced all you needed was a saddle, tank, engine, two wheels and the handlebar. I realized at once that the 851 Ducati"—Cagiva had taken over the Borgo Panigale firm—"was the utmost expression of technological reliability at the time. I had no wish to go back to the motorbikes of the past, my operation was not dictated by useless and ridiculous nostalgia. It was my intention to show that a touring bike ought to be as up-to-date as possible but not have an emphatically racing setup. So in the summer of '91 I took the running gear of the 851 together with the 904cc twin-valve air/oil-cooled engine of the 900GSC. This was the prototype of the M900, whose full name was to be the Monster. At Ducati you still hear it said that when some workers saw it for the first time, so boldly stated in the perimetral form of the frame supporting the power unit and surmounted by the massive fuel tank, they exclaimed, 'What a monster!' This may well be true but it's not the source of the name. My kids were small at the time and every day, when I got home, they used to clamor around me: 'Did you remember to by us some Monsters?'—those ferocious plastic creatures kids were crazy about then. I would toss them a few and they used to play happily with them. The name stuck in my mind, so when we were waiting for delivery of the prototype and Cagiva asked me what it was going to be called, I promptly replied 'Monster', and the name stuck. No one found anything more expressive …"

The significance of the Monster project was quite definitely the design and construction of a plaything for adults. The Monster amuses, fascinates, and stuns with its shamelessly explicit architecture, the display of its high-tech inner work-

The 851 gave Ducati buffs
the chance to imitate
the masterly riding on the
world's race circuits.

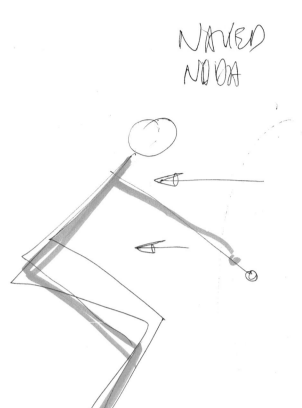

NAKED
NODA

1993, Monster
A sweet, seductive curve shapes the slightly swelling fuel tank, of notable size, then slides down, defining the edge of the saddle, and rises again to round off the tailpiece, which surmounts a jutting panel supporting the license plate and rear turn lights.

ings which make for completely safe and assured riding. The Monster taught us a new approach to biking, no longer based on rivalry between bike-owners, measured by speed, but a dialogue between the admirers of a shared lifestyle. The Monster is a fully achieved styling project. And while the visual impact is enthralling, the Monster also delivers the substance, with a heightened sense of technology reconciled with esthetic qualities. The M900 encouraged dialogue between its leisure-time aficionados. The centaurs in Walt Disney's *Fantasia* pursue one another joyously across the variegated landscape of hills to the notes of Beethoven's *Sixth Symphony*. Blaring motorcycle engines certainly can't compare in beauty with the horns of the *Pastoral*, but their shared playfulness creates a bond between them."

"On these warm summer nights," continues Miguel Galluzzi,

"I often ride down from the hills where I live to go and have a beer at one of those lakefront cafés. On the edge of the car parks, more than one Monster stands, making a fine show. You can always tell their owners among the occupants of the tables. There's no swank in them, even if they're youngsters, no desire to show off the superiority of the bike they own. They know they owe the pleasure it gives them to its safety, guaranteed by its mechanical efficiency. In this sense, truly, the Monster is the bike for bike-lovers, at least that's how I understood the project…"

"Naked or clothed?" was the title Fulvio Carmagnola gave his notes from the 1993 Motor Show published in *Modo*. "Perhaps it's too early to say this, but there seems to be a curious reversal of trend in motorcycle design. Modern design emerged as a sort of linear acceleration in the quest for form devoid of wind-resistance: in the thirties and forties streamlining acquired a symbolic value and even objects quite unconnected with speed were streamlined—floor polishers, fountain pens, blenders, and much else. It now seems that motorcycle form is retreating from this exaggerated symbolism and regressing toward archetypes of a different kind. In formal terms, at the recent EICMA Show in Milan, the Japanese technological avant-garde failed to present any innovations: it exhibited the variations on the usual forms, with fully faired styling or all-terrain bikes or imitations of the American custom-built models."

This epitomizes the fashion trends that so frustrated Miguel Galluzzi, when he worked for Honda's Design Center in Milan.

"The Monster bares itself,
passing from the extreme
of covering, total enclosure,
where power is signified
by arcane withdrawal, to the
open display of all its parts,
its mechanicals in full view."
Fulvio Carmagnola

"By contrast," continues Carmagnola, "the medium-high-powered European motorcycles embody a different trend, with a display of naked technology. It is as if the Europeans, tired of following the Japanese down the path of pure performance—which is anyway useless, except on a race track—had transformed the mechanicals themselves into a feature of style: the details of the engine, the frame, the arcane and now incomprehensible complexities of the structure, the suspension, that still delight the possessors of the old bikes—Guzzi, BSA, Matchless, Ajs, Norton and Harley—with their pipes, pistons, gearing, air intakes and vents, fins, radiators … Instead of being tucked away inside the hull of the fairing, they are exhibited as conspicuous technical forms slung from the frame. The fairing shrinks all the way to the absolute zero of nakedness. The exorbitant power of Japanese bikes is coyly concealed, at most signaled by the terrific decals scattered across their surfaces. The power of European and American bikes—more modest by definition—uses a different symbolic code: it is signaled by flaunting the mechanicals that create it. This trend—in taste and culture, a new market niche—is exemplified in the Triumphs but above all that brilliant local invention that is the Ducati Monster. Monster, as in *monstrare*, to show, its strangeness forcing it upon the gaze. The Monster bares itself, passing from the extreme of covering, total enclosure, where power is signified by arcane withdrawal, to the open display of

The intention of expressing power in a new way is evident because the Monster no longer signifies speed but safety, reliability: its forceful architecture flaunts the mechanicals, unprotected and unconcealed by any kind of armor.

all its parts, its mechanicals in full view. It is no accident that the lightweight lattice frame is the bike's most showy and formally effective feature. It is, perhaps, a return to the past, or rather a reinterpretation of it. From fluid dynamics to the mechanical, from the impure to the pure, where the symbolism displayed is the ancient symbolism of muscular force, of biking machismo, supremely exemplified by the Harley-Davidsons. What counts, ultimately, is not the power really experienced, used, but power as language, as forceful utterance. The Europeans have perhaps lighted upon a new way of saying all this."

Carmagnola's observations capture the distinctive quality of the Monster. The intention of expressing power in a new way is evident because, as Galluzzi points out, the Monster no longer signifies speed but safety, reliability. This is why its forceful architecture flaunts the mechanicals, unprotected and unconcealed by any kind of armor. The Monster's form has an immediate sensuous appeal. A sweet, seductive curve shapes the slightly swelling fuel tank, of notable size, then slides down, defining the edge of the saddle, and rises again to round off the tailpiece, which surmounts a jutting panel supporting the license plate and rear turn lights.

"In ergonomic terms," observes Massimo Bordi, "you can compare the styles of riding a bike to the way a rider sits his horse: either like a racing jockey, with stirrups shortened, pelvis pushed

The Monster's form
has immediate sensuous
appeal.

following pages
The Monster delivers
the substance: technology
reconciled with esthetic
qualities.

back and bust forward, or else lengthened stirrups with the pelvis brought forward and bust erect. The two positions correspond, roughly, to a bike's Sport and Touring set-ups. While the frontal S in the design of the Sport bike's fairing is lowered till the windshield is level with the rider's helmet, in a Touring bike it rises to shield the rider from the rush of air. In the naked bike, the fairing disappears, the rider is left unprotected. The bike's handling is easy at low and medium speed but it gets harder when you accelerate hard and at high speeds, where the pressure of the air tends to upset the rider's balance. The result is that the Monster displays a power that is not meant to be fully exploited. It owes its great success to exactly this feature. It is unrivaled in city traffic, it moves deftly and responds to the controls, favoring clear identification of obstacles by its lack of gadgetry. It shows to good advantage on the seafront on hot summer nights by the fullness of its forms matched with the unconcealed excellence of the mechanicals." So the Monster is a playtime bike and it measures up to playtime; no matter what

the occasion, it repays time lavished on it with the relish of adventure.

"Monster affirms a style and the style remains its enduring appeal," concluded Miguel Galluzzi. "The range of engine sizes presented, since that first M900 in 1993, has not affected its enchantment, now unchanged for more than seven years. This is undoubtedly the significance of the Monster, a motorcycle no longer confined to any frame of reference, the embodiment of advanced technology for the sake of safety in daily use. The future of the motorcycle, I believe, lies in the hands of designers who will increasingly focus on its playful significance. The motorcycle will come increasingly to represent the prize that crowns a desire long nurtured, which by its very nature can never be the satisfaction of a need. The motorcycle is not a means of transport; it is a plaything and playthings are chosen."

Galluzzi's arguments make the Monster the first bike that itself formed a market. In fact it created the niche, soon to be visited by all the big international motorcycle manufacturers.

"In making a survey of all the bikes that share Ducati's DNA," notes Marco Montemaggi, "I have to say that the Monster strikes me as like the island that pushes up above the waters, extraneous to them. From this consideration emerges the Monster's identity, as a bike that enshrines the experience of engines and chassises matured at Ducati, enhancing the legacy of that knowledge. This became even clearer when the Monster was recognized as the founder of a niche market, soon to be filled by Yamaha, Honda and Cagiva. I can certainly say that I myself ceded to its fascination and acquired one. It is my bike, generous, extraordinary, fantastic."

In quite a different field, the Monster's DNA is confirmed by Carlotta Cavalieri Ducati, a young biologist and Bruno's granddaughter. "A motorcycle finds its *raison d'être* only in movement, in that spatio-temporal dimension in which it is destined to confront the invisible but tenacious resistance of the air, which has modeled it in the course of years, compelling it gradually to shed its superfluous, angular lines, smoothing and softening them, making them more elegant, lowering the resistance of its form and heightening penetration. It is clearly not a mere esthetic evolution but a continuous and enthralling 'aerodynamic challenge' that at times acquires the features of a marvelous game invented for grownups. This game began the day that Neolithic man took

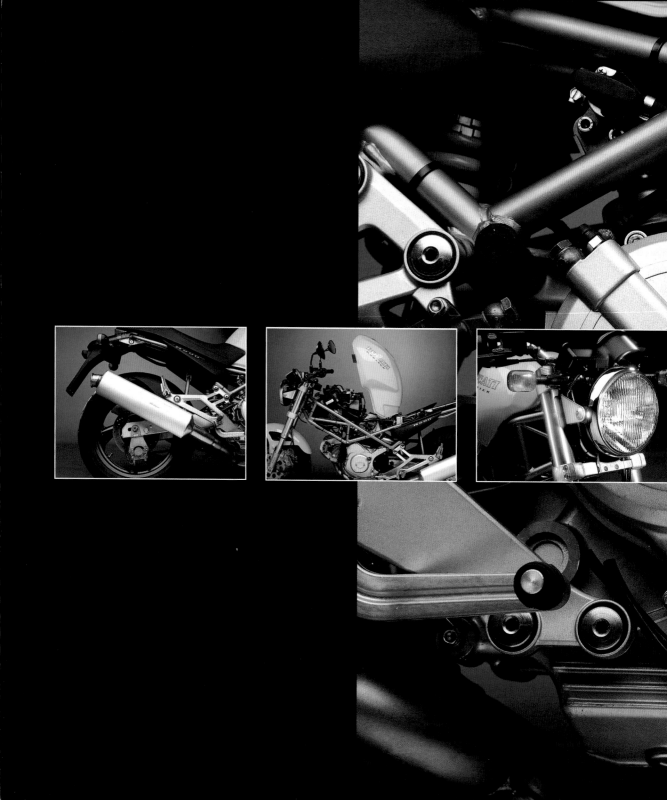

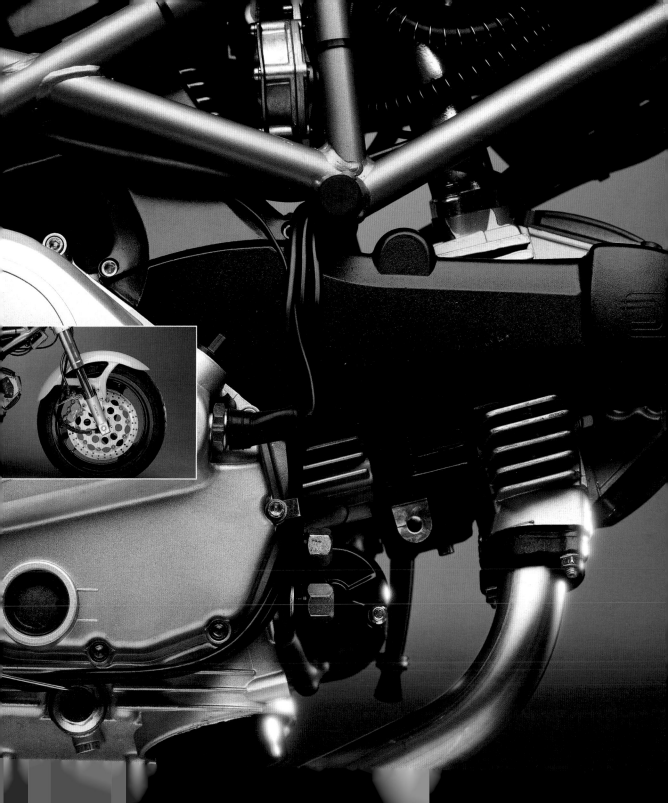

the trouble to invent the wheel. But is it then possible that he had to wait almost ten thousand years before intuiting that he could assemble two wheels one in front of the other and set them in movement to overcome their unstable equilibrium? Perhaps one of the first to give form to this intuition was Leonardo: his strange machines, foreshadowings of the future, which so impressed kings and princes, include the first bicycle, which no one could have built at that time. We had to wait till the end of the eighteenth century for the first bicycle to appear. Called the *cheval de bois*, it was a wooden contraption with two wheels linked by a crosspiece. The rider propelled it forward by pushing with his feet. Once before in the history of the collective imagination Homer had put wheels to a 'wooden horse,' the mythical Horse of Troy. And though the popular imagination may harbor a doubt as to whether this epic

horse ever really existed, we can exclude that we will ever see in nature an animal on wheels. This may appear self-evident but it is not really evident why we don't find mice-on-wheels or propeller-driven fishes. Since the most useful mechanisms of human transport have always been invented by nature, it is natural to ask why this should not be true of the most important form of human transport, the wheel. Long before man, animals and plants had invented combustion, flight, gliders, submarines, jet propulsion, parachutes

The Monster amuses, fascinates, stuns, with its shamelessly explicit architecture, the display of its high-tech inner workings which make for completely safe and assured riding.

Roberto Cavalli styles his
version of the Monster.

"Monster affirms a style and style remains its enduring appeal. The range of engine sizes since that first M900 in 1993, has not affected its enchantment, unchanged for more than seven years."
Miguel Galluzzi

and missiles. But the wheel, in the course of a long evolution, remains a purely human device: perhaps, even after thousands of years, the invention that man can boast of as his most authentic and exclusive.

"The reason no other living creatures have wheels, as illustrated in Jared Diamond's *The Biology of the Wheel*, lies in friction. A tiny pebble would be quite enough to stop an imaginary mouse on wheels. Practically every kind of animal has to traverse rugged terrain and cope with continuous obstacles; but even if it simply wanted to move over a fairly smooth surface it would still need very big wheels. Our big 'error' of wheels has been made possible by the fact that we live in a world carpeted with roads. Moreover all living structures need to be supplied with energy, they need oxygen. A wheel needs a pivot or hub, but the pivot would be an obstacle to the transport of energy, though it is true there do exist parts of animals that are not irrigated with blood. So, even though in the scale of energy swimming costs less than flying, which costs less than walking, at parity of mass, a man on a bicycle remains perhaps the most economical form of transport. In this case evolution was unable to select the most convenient form in terms of energy-efficiency because it was limited by constraints of form and function. The same rigorous parameters of form and function underlie the choices of engineers, physicists and designers as they labor to improve a new model motorbike. In short, the evolution from the Cucciolo to the Monster can be seen through the eyes of the great evolutionists, who maintain that the forms of living creatures are the result not just of a process of invention but of a progressive adaptation of existing forms."

A wonderful synthesis, the Ducati motorcycles combine the process of invention with the progressive adaptation of existing forms. "But 1993 was not just the year of the Monster," notes Marco Montemaggi. "Pierre Terblanche also designed and built the Supermono, a bike intended exclusively for racing. For the first time the competition machine was no longer an exclusive part of Ducati's traditional engineering school but also embodied the study of form, an added value. The design was decisive in the Supermoto, which boasted an engine designed by Massimo Bordi with the assistance of the project director Claudio Domenicali."

The bike is not just beautiful, explains Marco Masetti. "The Sound of Singles race formula offered the designers numerous cues, since the only limitation was the number of cylinders: one. For the rest, absolute freedom. This is a class where artisan-mechanics re-develop production machines with inspired new approaches, but where a design engineer like Massimo Bordi also falls for the allure of the one-cylinder bike. Legend has it that the idea crystallized in his mind one hot summer day when he was stuck in traffic in a car without air-conditioning. Bordi sketched out the design, adding a very advanced technical feature: a twin-cam big end with four desmo valves, liquid cooling and an ingenious system to annul vibrations by means of an auxiliary shaft. The idea was entrusted to Domenicali as the project engineer and his staff, who carried out the execution and also designed the running gear, while the designer Pierre Terblanche tackled the fairing and the bike's esthetics. The result was one of the finest pure sports bikes ever made, with running gear in authentic Ducati style and very compact dimensions … There are details over which one wants to linger all day—for instance the splendid aluminum forks with a truss at the top, or the absolutely unmistakable line of the Racing spirit … In the races it was entrusted to a number of riders, from the British journalist Alan Cathcart to

Lucchiari, and proved clearly it was one of the finest and most competitive single-cylinder bikes ever built, though the engine size, at 550cc, was rather on the small side compared to its rivals."

In the Supermono Livio Lodi glimpses the spark of that innovatory spirit that was to inform the future of the Ducati project. "If the Monster can be referred to no category of the past in the case history of motorcycle manufacturing in general, unless we relate it at Ducati to the Scrambler, whose flexibility and explicit architecture of the mechanicals it renewed, with Terblanche the Supermono hit the bull's eye of that eminence, racing, where engineering competence is still jealously defended. The fact that design enters into a dialogue with the technical dimension made Supermono in 1993 a real breakthrough at Ducati."

Pierre Terblanche told me: "I instantly fell in love with Ducati bikes in 1974 when I first saw the 750 GT designed in 1971 by Fabio Taglioni. Seven years later, in 1981, I was able to buy one. I rode it for a long time and it gave me incommensurable emotions. At Cape Town, where I was born, I studied Graphic Design and I worked as Art Director for a big advertising firm. After this experience, which brought me into touch with the leading European manufactures, who wanted to promote their products in South Africa, I decided to go to Europe. Sponsorship by Ford Germany enabled me to take a Master's degree in Transport Design in London, where design covers all forms of transport, by land, sea and sky. Then I worked in Germany for six years at Volkswagen's Experimental Center, up to 1989. Finally I decided to work with Massimo Tamburini in Rimini. I wanted to fulfill my urge to design motorcycles I needed to gain experience in the atelier of a master. I was enthralled by the beauty of the Paso Ducati, which Tamburini designed and built in 1986. To me design means a synergic rapport with your client. Both sides have to be quite clear about their objective. In the case of the Supermono project, when I was already Director of Design at Ducati, the objective was a bike for racing, meaning racing better. So the result couldn't be just an esthetic value. Here the design defines the racing function, in synergy with the engineering. The two sides can't be understood separately, as they so often are. Design can only be a harmony of skills united by the same final aim. The Supermono was a first test case at Ducati, even though a motorbike fairing is the simplest to give a shape to, when you're less concerned to order the components concealed by the fairing. With the Supermono I tried to express the integra-

But the Monster is an extreme machine only for those who understand the essence of pleasure.

tion of the fundamental features of the sports category, in a kind of reinterpretation, which I translated into a more evolved form than that of its predecessors."

Even hoisting it onto its centerstand doesn't freeze the sense of movement. Motionless, the Supermono still declares its motorial intentions. The focus of this effect lies in the splendid aluminum forks, which seem to give the whole upper framework a forward thrust, while the thrust absorbers, banded and stowed under the tail, stand out at the side. The fuel tank is set up against the trestle frame, emphasizing the sharply raked angle of its design and looking as if it was slung above the saddle. Tank, saddle and tail form a sort of broken line with a syncopated profile. The fairing enwraps and sheathes the mechanicals, with its upper edge forming the line of the cockpit, in perfect counter-harmony to the design above. The bike evokes immediate comparison with the animal world. Not all racehorses are beautiful, more than one thoroughbred disappoints the esthetic canons. In this case the Supermono is a thoroughbred whose beauty definitely corresponds to the soundness of its legs.

"The Supermono is an absolute example of the design of the extreme machine," comments Marco Montemaggi, "a synergic design, in which pure research bears fruit in the definition of the most beautiful single-cylinder bike ever made for racing. Its limit, however, lies in its cost, which prevents it from being translat-

ed into a prototype, a production model. So apart from the few that were made for races, the Supermono remains a great achievement in the history of Ducati, securely a precious rarity for those collectors fortunate enough to own one. But Ducati wanted a model capable of embodying the legacy of the 851 and derivatives. The Monster paid homage to the perfect running assembly of Bordi's legendary machine, but the very nature of this felicitous design excluded it from the line of inheritance, the development of its outstanding racing qualities. In 1994 the 916 riveted and enthralled Ducati fans and gave them many a sleepless night, as well as leaving the world's big motorcycle manufacturers breathless. A fellow countryman of mine, Massimo Tamburini, crazy as only a Romagnolo can be, great, perhaps the greatest of living motorbike designers, worked the miracle."

The 916 came onto the market in the years of the closest rapport between Ducati and Cagiva. "We were a motorcycle group," comments Massimo Bordi, "and so we exploited the synergies between the two marques and found ourselves part of a company that was then planning to re-launch itself and had a strong distribution network. We became great in that period also thanks to the enthusiasm and passion of the company's owners. Then the limitations began to emerge: the Group was committed on too many different and

1993, Supermono
"For the first time the competition machine was no longer an exclusive part of Ducati's traditional engineering school but embodied the study of form, an added value."
Marco Montemaggi

following pages
With the Supermono I tried to express the integration of the fundamental features of the sports category through a reinterpretation in a more evolved form than its predecessors."
Pierre Terblanche

SUPERMONO
DESMOQUATTRO

challenging fronts with a difficult financial situation. Now that, finally, Ducati belonged 49% to Cagiva and 51% to the Texas Pacific Group (an American investment fund), the conditions existed to re-launch the firm toward the objectives it merited."

The whole Ducati packet soon passed into the hands of the Texas Pacific Group and on March 24, 1999, the shares were quoted on the Stock Exchange.

Four years after the 916's debut, on June 26, 1998, an exhibition, "The Art of the Motorcycle," opened at New York's Solomon R. Guggenheim Museum. It caused quite a stir, attracted a lot of comment in the press, and drew a wide international public. The following month Benedetta Pignatelli wrote in *Specchio*, the supplement to *La Stampa* in Turin: "5431 visitors flocked to the show on the third of July to gaze at over 100 motorcycles and 130 years of history. A record for the Fourth of July holiday weekend. 'The best thing in New York right now. A must for anyone seriously interested in art and design,' enthused the poet Frederick Seidel in the *Wall Street Journal*. In *Going Fast* Seidel had devoted a poem titled *Milan* to a 1999 Ducati 916 speeding down Via Borgospesso: 'Massimo Tamburini's red Ducati 916 is a Donatello sculpture mediated by Brancusi. An extraordinary combination of esthetics and functionalism,' he wrote."

So in a poet's imagination the 916 is a work of art, the nearest possible approach to the supreme art of Donatello (1386–1460), who revived the art of ancient statuary through free-standing sculptural forms in a restless, highly personal interpretation. But it is also a work of art mediated by a striving for pure form, stripped of accessory attributes, of the kind that characterizes the creative development of Constantin Brancusi (1871–1957). Rather more judiciously, Gillo Dorfles in the *Corriere della Sera* observed: "This is not the first time that the grave dilemma whether design is art or just technology has cropped up. And probably it will not be the last. Yet a little common sense can help us make up our minds. In this case it is nothing less than the celebrated and hallowed Spiral at New York's Solomon R. Guggenheim Museum—the work of the great Frank Lloyd Wright—disfigured say some, enhanced claim others (so the *Herald Tribune* informs us) by a big exhibition devoted to motorbikes: 'The Art of the Motorcycle.' So there are some who hold that these machines deserve an exhibition, true, but at most in a museum of design or motoring, while others—who also invoke the literary side of the exhibition (see the case of the film *Easy Rider* and the fact that the MoMA also exhibits examples of industrial design)—defend its artistic exhibition as an authentic Icon of our Time. And I too believe that the motorcycle is one of the most extraordinary icons of the twentieth century: a divinity (alas sacrilegious) of speed, of the spark, of dynamism. And even more I believe that often the bodywork of a motorcycle contains in itself elements of sculptural involvement even superior to those of an automobile. In short: let's welcome the motorcycle to the no longer so very sacred Guggenheim, provided there is no attempt to get the public to believe that it is the equivalent of a target by Jasper Johns or a jam jar by Robert Rauschenberg or Claes Oldenburg's gigantic tube of toothpaste, because it is as well that a minimum gap between pop art and design should be maintained."

1994, 916
"It enthralled Ducati fans and gave them many a sleepless night, as well as leaving the world's big motorcycle manufacturers breathless."
Marco Montemaggi

following pages
"Massimo Tamburini's red Ducati 916 is a Donatello sculpture mediated by Brancusi. An extraordinary combination of esthetics and functionalism."
Frederick Seidel

Ennio Caretto, writes again in the *Corriere della Sera*: "The *New York Times* splashed the exhibition on the front page but highlighted the complaints of the traditionalists. Steven Mazoh, the gallery owner who supplies Croesuses like Walter Annenburg with their masterpieces, suggested to the Guggenheim that if its aim is to sell more tickets all it needs to do is offer visitors free admission to Coney Island. From Don

Imus, a celebrated disk jockey, comes a reverse criticism: 'What's going on? The motorcycle is the symbol of contestation, transgression, and now it's been co-opted by the establishment.' One viewer phoned in to the culture channel on TV: 'The Museum's director ought to expel these people like Jesus expelled the merchants from the temple.' This is the last

thing the director in question, Thomas Krens, is likely to do. 'The Art of the Motorcycle' is his brainchild, he devised and curated it. 'Motorcycles,' retorted Krens in the *New York Times*, 'express more than anything else contemporary fears, dangers and fantasies: they are artistic symbols.' "
Benedetta Pignatelli concluded: "The exhibition celebrates two-wheelers for their design, their technical efficiency, and their role as cultural icons. 'The motorcycle represents many themes of this century: technology, speed, rebellion, transformation—according to the words of Krens … The nineties call for rigor … The Japanese keep their heads above water on the market because of the solid foundations they laid in the eighties. There is a forceful return of the Italians, who go through magical cyclical phases, first in the fifties, partly in the seventies and now in the nineties. Two names above all: Miguel Galluzzi, the Argentine designer who invented the mythical Ducati Monster (1993), almost a grunge bike, and Massimo Tamburini who designed the Ducati 916

"The 916 at once began its racing career by winning the world championship SBK 1994, 1995, 1996 and 1998 as well as an impressive number of Italian titles."
Marco Masetti

following pages
The sinuous, powerful cluster of the exhaust pipes projects from the fairing at the tail, uniting the manifold below the womb-shaped saddle.

... Ultan Gulfoyle, Krens's curatorial advisor, confirms the return of the passion for motorbikes: 'There's a renewed desire for a respite from responsibility, the family, kids, wives and husbands. And in some countries there's a use of the motorcycle as a means of locomotion that replicates the postwar period ... In the future I foresee the use of the motorbike as a way of having fun, now that the baby-boomers can finally afford it. And a real rapprochement between women and two-wheelers, already evident in recent years.'"

In 1998 two Ducati models, diametrically opposed in the significance of their projects, the Monster and the 916, together crowned the summit of the spiral that forms the gallery circuit at Frank Lloyd Wright's celebrated New York museum.

"There is no need to be connoisseurs of esthetics or diehard Ducati fans to admit it," declares Marco Masetti, "but quite incredibly the 916 (and its derivatives that are still racing and winning today and constitute the top of the Ducati range) will go down in history as an immensely concrete bike."

From a cognoscente of the engineering tradition this observation is definitely worthy of attention, especially if it refers to a model that owes much of its success to the extraordinary intuitions of the Romangolo designer.

"Behind the 916 there is the genius of Massimo Tamburini, a true Renaissance man," continues Masetti, "who has known how to unite intuition, technical ability and a love of beauty that are rarely found together in one man. Tamburini had already built great motorcycles like the Paso, the Cagiva Mito 125 and, before he became the head of an independent facility in San Marino, he had created the Bimota. At Ducati in the late eighties he was given the order: design a motorbike with a tubular frame and two-cylinder twin-cam engine. Tamburini went well beyond an exercise in styling (so foreign to his character) and around that engine he created a work of art. The running gear grew around a tubular trestle frame with a diameter of 28 cen-

996

timeters, with single-strut forks cast in aluminum. But Tamburini wanted to go farther: he understood, for example, that an engine like the Ducati needed a large-capacity air-box and he made it, using all the space available, with the lower part of the fuel tank as a cover and shaping the fluting in the structure of the chassis. Not yet satisfied, he designed the most beautiful bodywork seen on a sports bike in the last ten years. The 916 at once began its racing career by winning the world championship SBK 1994, 1995, 1996 and 1998 as well as an impressive number of Italian titles."

So it is no accident if the Monster and the 916 stand at the top of the Guggenheim Spiral. The two models are highly symbolic examples in which design truly means the design of the totality of the object and this, as the competition subsequently showed, not just at Ducati. The 916 was an extreme machine in the hands of Carl Fogarty, who won no fewer than four titles on it, as well as in the hands of those who, without taking part in races, sought the essence of competitiveness in the color, form and content of a bike. But the Monster was an extreme machine only for those who understand the essence of pleasure.

So it is not the models that embody a design so much as the different lifestyles that justify its presence, and this is the true symbolic significance of Ducati design in the new century. The inspired insights of Massimo Tamburini encounter the expectations, never quelled, of those instinctively led toward a more competitive style of life, in continuous quest of symbols to confirm its formal and substantial quality. A symbolic synthesis of achieved technical and esthetic conciliation, of accomplished hardware-software excellence, the 916 asserts itself as the thesis of Ducati's incessant refinement of design. It has no kin among faired motorbikes, since in sport bikes the fairing is an addition, cladding to reduce air resistance, protecting the mechanicals that establish their identity, like armor sheathing their powerful muscles as mechanical warriors in full battle array. But the shell of the 916 interprets the totality of the machine, enhances it, heightens it, optimizes its performance, and is therefore inseparable from the mechanicals, is born conjoined with them.

The design of the air-box is exemplary, where the form resolves the need to draw in the maximum amount of flow. The large surface of the air-box is surmounted by the double dials of the instrument panel, cut out of the base of the cockpit, which is aligned below the fuel tank with the peak of the tail. The sinuous, powerful cluster of the exhaust

The design of the air-box is exemplary: the design ensures maximum air-flow.

following pages
The shell interprets the totality of the machine, enhances it, heightens it, optimizes its performance, and is therefore inseparable from the mechanicals, is born conjoined with them.

pipes projects from the fairing at the tail, uniting the manifold below the womb-shaped saddle. The frame of trestle steel tubing supports the mechanicals, fitting flush into the fairing on the front and rear tele-hydraulic forks, which grip its massive wheels like talons.

Massimo Tamburini probably dreamt of building the 916, even before beginning to design it, like Piero and Nando in Donatello Bellomo's fine story, *L'uomo che cavalcava un sogno*. "That day Nando arrived at the workshop at six sharp but the wooden outer door was shut. Piero was out. He opened the padlock, switched on the hotplate, filled the coffeepot, laid out the tools on the workbench, wiped them with a rag and checked that the double spares of tires and inner tubes, sprinkled with talc, were all in readiness. At six-thirty he loaded the pickup. He was about to load the gas drum when the sun spread over the concrete shiny with oil and illuminated the sheet that covered the Bulon. Nando was easily moved by that motorbike, shaped with his hands, and was so stirred that like an automaton he had to obey the

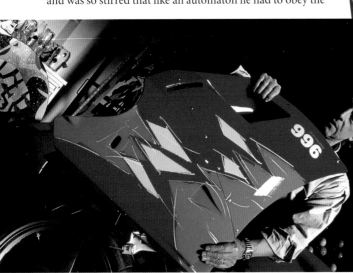

velvety voice whispering 'uncover me.' A cup of coffee in his hand, he slipped the canvas down over the handlebars and fuel tank, hypnotized by the reflections on the chromed cheeks. He didn't hear the Frera shifting gears across the canal or the double vroom that his cousin gave the bike before cutting the engine. Bikes are beautiful as women and they don't get in your hair, he thought. He didn't hear Piero when entered and went straight to the coffeepot, or when he

swore at the cup he had spilt on the hob. He only stirred when the heavy hand clasped his shoulder: 'Sorry to be late, Nando, but I couldn't leave the job half done.' 'You did the right thing. But you stink like a whore of jasmine. That's quite a bruise you've got on your neck. The widow was in form, eh?' Piero said nothing. He took the cup of coffee and gulped it down. It was seven o'clock and they had to be moving."

From Busto they go to Monza where, "For an hour Piero lived like a lion. The Bulon took the circuits with such a full massive melody that it sounded like Tamagno. He had no need to look at his stop-watch to see he was

going fast. Lying flat against the fuel tank, his knees gripping the chromed cheeks, he hit the trajectories, going faster at every passage. 'Racing a bike is easy. You just have to learn how to do the curves. Everyone looks good on a straight …' A hundred yards before the stands he leaned his cheek to the track and stretched out along the frame like a lizard in the sun. He caught a glimpse of Nando taking the times and kept the throttle open, floating into the wake of a Gilera 350V after overtaking a Norton that had just left the pits."

The Poderosa II that was the traveling companion of Alberto Granada and Ernesto Che Guevara in the nineteen-fifties could hardly boast the reliability of its ancestor.

"The Norton bore down on him at the entrance to the broad left-hand bend. Piero took it sharply: between the Bulon and the grass there was no more than eighteen inches, but the Norton slipped through effortlessly and designed a trajectory that seemed to have been drawn with a pair of compasses. Piero tried to keep up but the Norton was running on rails, gaining yard after yard while he and the Bulon were already pushed to the limit. He pulled into the pits and let his eyes follow the rider, who was now handing the bike over to his mechanic. He pushed away Nando, who was hugging him with the stopwatch in hand, and removed his helmet. 'Who's that guy?' Nando thrust a timesheet into his hand. 'You're a wonder. Just look at this. And what a bike, it's like an arrow.' He got off the saddle and stood looking at the guy with the Norton, who was lighting a cigarette and joking with three women. Blue eyes, medium height, long slick hair brushed back. 'Who's that guy?' he repeated. Nando shrugged his shoulders and muttered, 'Can't say. He drives a big car with a Novara license plate. Someone with money.' Piero rummaged in his pocket and took out a bedraggled cigarette. 'No, he's a wonder. Believe you me.' He had no time to light the ragged Macedonia because the guy in the light-blue overalls offered him a Camel from a gold cigarette case. 'May I introduce myself? I'm Achille Varzi, of Galliate.'"

Ugo Nespolo's
styling of the 996.

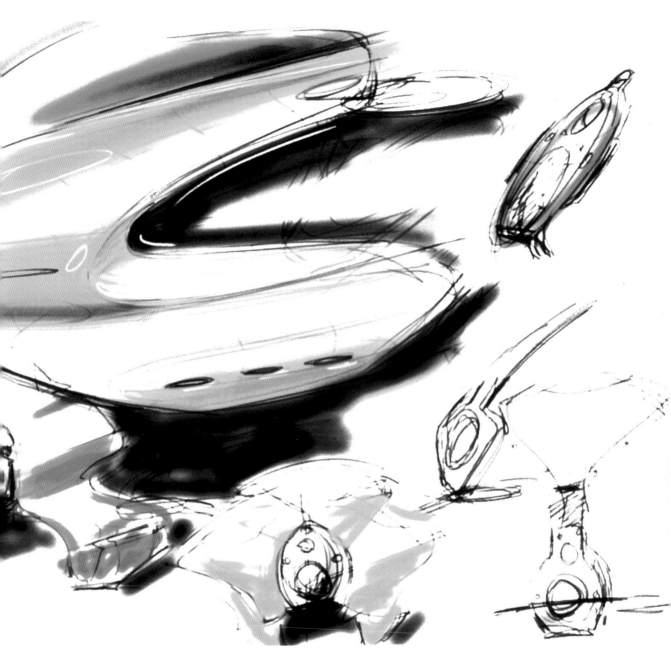

2000, MH900e
In Pierre Terblanche's
design, "memory and
evolution are manifested
as signs of emotion."
Livio Lodi

Varzi pays homage to Piero and Nando's dream. That Varzi who, like his great rival Tazio Nuvolari, would soon abandon motorcycles for auto racing, always wearing his impeccable pure silk overalls.

With the 916 Massimo Tamburini realized the dream of those youngsters who still today, though not taking part in races, see a motorbike as the essence of competition and are happy to share the thrill with champions like Fogarty.

Pierre Terblanche, on the other hand, evokes the memory of Mike Hailwood: a great rider, a hero of the perilous circuit on the Isle of Man back in 1978, when he rode a Ducati 900SS, the daughter of Fabio Taglioni's mythical 750 GT, to mark the debut of the Mhe, a production sport bike that pays homage in the year 2000 to that legendary motorcycle. "Wandering around the museum with an attentive eye, as a true fan of the Ducati epic," recounts Marco Montemaggi, "Pierre Terblanche pauses in front of the mock-up of the 900SS, which served more than twenty years as the model for Hailwood's bike. Why not combine memory with today's technology but with all its fascination unchanged, in a model that most enhances its coloring, that red and gray that was Ducati's livery at the time. This reflection gave rise to the MH900e, the Mark Hailwood 900 evolution. Terblanche's decision to state fully the architecture of the mechanicals has nothing to do with a retro design operation: in fact it stresses and confirms the technological advance of the whole machine."

Livio Lodi observes: "Memory and evolution are manifested as signs of emotion. We have all noticed it in Ducati. Hence the top management's decision to entrust Internet with the task of communicating the significance of the operation. In a few days the bookings outstripped the most optimistic expectations. The MH900e immediately found its niche."

In effect Internet acts as the immediate vector of a significance which goes well beyond the object present to the attention, which even justifies it appearance. Today motorcycles that are both beautiful and fast are no longer exclusive to the fans of Japanese bikes, and this is shown by those fans of Japanese bikes who do not hesitate to prefer a Honda to a Suzuki, or vice versa, when one or the other tops the appeal ratings. The MH900e appeals to a much more refined palate. It heightens the attention, reawakens the senses of those who want to understand the reasons behind a design, who want to know it is in perfect harmony with the history of its maker, for its

"Design is an operation
of unveiling and
perpetuation. And since
form circumscribes the
object, it embodies a minute
part of nature, as in the
human body: the object
is fundamentally
anthropomorphic."
Jean Baudrillard

greater credibility. Ducati fans recognize the authenticity of a Ducati bike, because Ducatis always correspond to the authenticity of the lifestyle of the Ducati fans.

The presentation states: "The heart of the MH900e is the L-shaped two-cylinder 900cc with twin desmo valves that has defined Ducati's style ever since the 1960s, when a couple of prototypes of the Ducati 750SS stunned the motorcy-

cling world by taking first and second place at the Imola 200 Mile Race. Completely open, the MH900e's engine seems to float in mid-air ... It is cradled by the legendary chrome-molybdenum trestle frame painted red. The unique single-strut tubular forks are connected directly to the engine, heightening the bike's light, buoyant look. The picture is completed by the fairing, with its superb, sinuous forms…"

Pierre Terblanche explains the significance of the term

Mock-up and prototypes
of the MH900e.
"The Ducatis of the past were
distinguished for lightness,
simplicity, directness. The MH900e
possesses those same qualities,
but is the fruit of a far more complex
technological groundwork."
Pierre Terblanche

design when applied to motorcycles as objects: "It is design in its totality, not just the outer shell, as is often supposed. This doesn't mean that a single designer can claim to be capable of handling the whole design job. Rather it means that the design has to be unified, and it has to draw on all the forces identified with it, in a community of intents, to ensure the best outcome. This is the meaning of the term design. Designing a motorcycle today means working outward from the inside of the machine, because the most difficult thing is to give shape and order to the volumes formed by the mechanicals. For the first time at Ducati, the design of the MH900e entailed the use of software that controlled the bike as a whole, no longer just the definition of its power assembly.

And this is an important fact, confirming the uniqueness of the project, where the phases of design were not based on

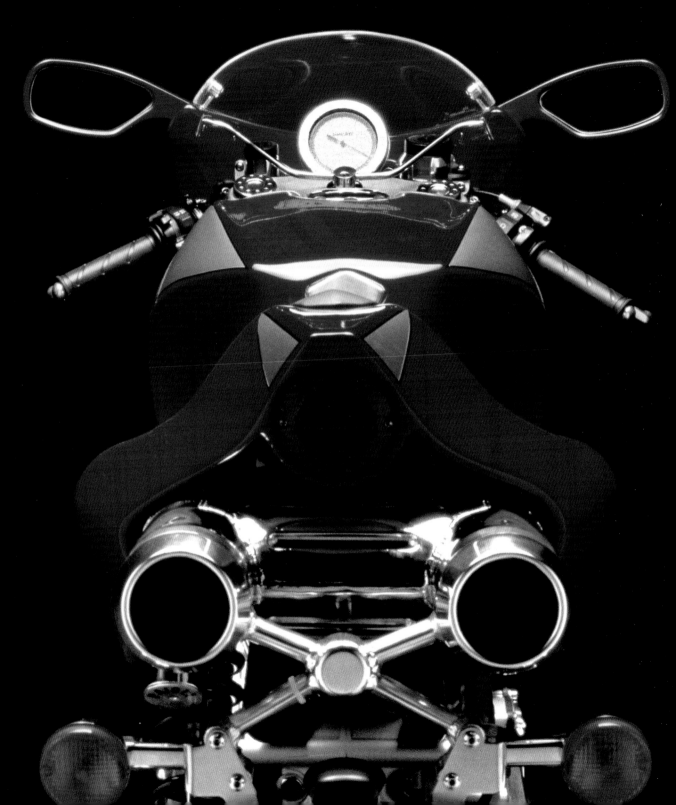

different skills, but rather the different skills had to find a
way to express themselves fully. Once defined virtually, the
model takes concrete shape through the gradual evolution
of prototypes that will enable the product to go into production in the arc of two years. As an object, the MH900e
avoids overstaying, the temptation of looking too groomed
both in the details and overall, because the aim was to avoid
the least trace of a facile mannerism. The Ducatis of the
past were distinguished by their lightness, compactness,
simplicity and directness. The MH900 is distinguished
today for those same qualities, but is the fruit of a far more
complex technological groundwork."

In *The System of Objects*, Jean Baudrillard writes: "In the creation or manufacture of objects, man, by imposing a form
that is cultural, transubstantiates nature: the filiation of substances, from age to age, from form to form, institutes the
original scheme of creativity: creation *ab utero*, with all the
poetic and metaphoric symbolism that accompanies it.
Meaning and value derive from the hereditary
transmission of substances under the juris-
diction of form: therefore the world is
experienced as given (in the unconscious
and during childhood this sensation
remains), and design is an operation of
unveiling and of perpetuation. And, since
form circumscribes the object, in it is
included a minute part of nature, as in the
human body: the object is fundamentally
anthropomorphic."

Extraordinary, beyond the bounds of the
normal, commonly recognized meaning
for a simple means of transport: the
motorcycle. It is, before we can call it a
means, a way, the most representative, therefore a symbol of mobility, a game within
the game. That is how Terblanche confirmed once again, in 2001, the excellence of

that way, configuring the most accessible means to testing. The Multistrada is not an extreme machine, nor could it be called a genuine touring bike. It is a Ducati through and through, but it appears "saddled with long stirrups" for easy, controlled handling. It favors the forward, upright riding position.

"Ducati needed an easy-to-manage motorbike for the ordinary person who is not bothered by vague competitive ambitions or a desire to imitate our champions. A requirement, as Terblanche noted, of which I was also aware but had not succeeded in satisfying. After the Monster, the Multistrada is the best selling bike, indicating its appeal today to that niche of potential consumers who are indifferent initially to the lure of a brand. The Multistrada is a sport bike, a Superbike, but designed to provide the comfort of an armchair. I finalized the plan to create a motorbike for everyday use that expressed its playful essence in a formal and essential accessibility, capable of tackling all road conditions: mountains, plains and motorways. I took particular care with the positioning of the seat and fuel tank: a body shell by all means. The windshield, with its curved shape, is attached to the large raised handlebars and the fork so as to follow better the movement of direction changes with very tight turning circles. The fuel tank stretches underneath the seat whereas in the front section there is a compartment for objects such as glasses, gloves and roadmaps. Even if a single detail of the motorbike does not seem innovative, as does the concept, it is not restricted to a particular use. The Multistrada is universal. If anyone asks me: 'Is that not perhaps a limitation?' I reply that the limitation, if anything, is that the motorbikes fulfil a single function ..."

In *The Infinite Passion*, a book published in 2004, for the ninetieth issue of the magazine *Motociclismo*: "The Multistrada wrong foots all the others somewhat thanks to its design midway between track and enduro and to its anabolic supermotard proportions. When a chance to try it comes along, all doubts disappear immediately: one of the most enjoyable motorbikes ever seen for everyday use was created at Borgo Panigale. What's more, special attention has been given to travel needs: a place for saddlebags and a GPS, a good size fuel tank and adjustable headlights. It has an air-cooled 90° L twin-cylinder four-stroke engine; tubular steel trestle frame; suspension: Shawa front fork and single-sided rear fork in light alloy with progressive linkage; lastly, 5-spoke light alloy wheel rims; double floating disk front brake, single disk rear brake."

Livio Lodi noted, "A few kilometres from the Ducati factory a road was built that began at Bologna, wound its way to the top of the Tuscan-Emilian Apenines, then continued on to Florence. The name of the road is Passo della Futa and at one time it was a legendary course for bikers from Emilia-Romagna. The road presented a severe challenge: tight bends, hairpin curves, extended bends, turns taken at full speed and at 180°. For most of the first 50 kilometers, the road surface was uniform and like a racetrack. With one knee on the ground and eyes fixed on the road, they took on the most difficult bends. Then the surface changed: damp in the shaded areas and full of holes on the curves. For a long

time at Ducati they had dreamt of a motorbike that could take on the Passo della Futa. That bike was the Multistrada 1000 DS, a high-performance sport bike, perfect for all types of asphalt, from the smooth and uniform to the rough and bumpy. It was designed to be used with the same ease on tortuous roads, large motorways and in congested city traffic. I often stop to look at the motorbikes set on a 'carousel' in the museum, chasing each other, one after the other. It is a curious, pleasant feeling, similar to what we experience when leafing slowly through a family album of photographs. Among those pictures we see the faces of persons long since departed, and yet still living and near in our recollection, particularly when they remind us of happy memories. The sensation becomes stronger if I find myself in front of some old 750 F1s, the last project of Fabio Taglioni, and the first 851s that won the Superbike titles in the 1990s. I feel myself becoming a museum object, but my annoyance passes when, at the end of the carousel, with the motorbikes chasing after each other with an almost unstoppable rhythm, I see the latest competition models that immortalized Ducati's epic achievements in the racing world. Terblanche was entrusted with the far from easy task of designing a motorbike capable of challenging a myth: Tamburini's 916 (996). The 999, from the year 2002, is an example of a design aimed at an esthetic-technical reconciliation of seemingly disparate components. Among these, is the ergonomics factor for less tiring, stress-free motorcycling. Equipped with a 90° L twin-cylinder "Testastretta" engine, water-cooled and using an electronic injection-ignition system, with 4 valves and dual camshaft, it capitalizes on the technical and fluid-dynamic concepts at the forefront of the motorcycling world.

For the dedicated biker there is always the Desmodromic system of valve control, which guarantees smooth distribution in every situation. The innovative asymmetrical layout of the exhaust system and the high-volume mono muffler have improved significantly the coupling of intermediate systems. In keeping with the Ducati tradition, the frame is a high-resistance tubular steel trestle with an elevated limit of yield. The light and highly resistant dual-sided fork is in earth-fused aluminum. The clutch and front brake levers and the rear brake pedal are adjustable."

Michele Lupi wrote in *Racers*: "The best riders of the AMA

(American Motorcycle Association) championship go on to the Mondiale and sometimes they win it, like the Australian Troy Bayliss of the Ducati team." Bayliss won the race with the 998, the latest model in the development of the series that was launched by the 916, which preceded, in Ducati's evolutionary curve, the arrival of the 999. His judgement on this next point is no less authoritative. "It is fundamental," he declares, "for a rider to be able to establish the right symbiosis with his bike. This presupposes the possibility of adjusting the riding position. The Ducati 999 allows for the foot rests to be set in five different positions to ensure the correct position of the legs. Moreover in order to adjust the rider's seat correctly for the race track, it is possible, in the single seat version, to shift the position of the combination seat and fuel tank horizontally by 20 millimetres, which allows for the same adjustment for the arms and knees."

Terblanche noted, "The 998 was in fact a race-track bike, not easy to use on the roads, very hard suspension, position of the rider decidedly uncomfortable, excessive strain on the forearms. It was suited to short runs rather than long ones. For someone like myself, whose height is over 1.75 meters, I could not ride it in relative comfort; someone shorter would not be able to climb onto the seat due to its raised position. I took on the task of designing a hyper sport bike with deci-

dedly innovative features, because in the Ducati tradition, a motorbike conceived for the road enters the track to win the Superbike category, clearly distinguishing itself from the Grand Prix models. The riders are the first to pay their compliments. Ben Bostrom exclaimed: 'At last a motorbike I can ride for twenty-five laps with total commitment without getting tired.' Michele Lupi explains, "For the Superbike, two parallel championships: one is the American national AMA, origin of the species, and the other is the Mondiale, organized by Octagon Motor Sport of the Flammini brothers, today known as the Flammini Group. A single encounter: the annual showdown, mid-July, when the two championships take place on a fiery weekend at Laguna Seca for the American stage of the world championship. The sweltering heat and burning sun are only a breath of wind away from elegant Carmel and Monterey. In 1999, two strapping young lads with long sideburns, piercing gazes and Ducati plates decided to prove to everyone that the AMA riders were no less capable than the aces of the Mondiale. Mr. Anthony Gobert and Mr. Ben Bostrom came in victorious in both of the two Sunday races. Ducati saw in Ben Bostrom, with his surfer's physique and hand on the gas, a true champion, a shining testimonial and brought him over to Europe where, after a somewhat chequered fir-

2002, 999

A living example
of feasibility for a model
extreme in its performance,
but suited to the rider's
comfort.

999 : "To indicate the dual
purpose of the motorbike,
I inserted turn lights
in the side mirrors, easily
removable, when moving
from road to track."
Pierre Terblanche

st year, he began winning the hearts of the fans over …"
The 999 responds well today to the consummate handling skill of the rider. "Years ago," continued Terblanche, "the fascination of the motorbike was mainly about its difficult handling and this gave the rider an opportunity to show off his ability to dominate this or that model. Today that is just a romantic memory from the past. The Japanese produce motorbikes for wide consumption. There is no difference in their machines—they have to please everyone. Our bikes cannot possibly please everyone, because the design is a plan within a plan with a distinct Ducati identity. The study of the 999 shape is intimately connected to its aerodynamic, mechanical and electronic function. The constituent parts are not separate entities, but are perfectly integrated, the result of optimization of all the innovative resources. Planning a motorcycle does not mean joining single parts created at different times, but rather to breathe life into a synergetic co-operation of the components, which must integrate perfectly with a single important, and even symbolic, objective. In designing the shape of the 999 I interpreted the cockpit in a very tapered form; the fairing lowe-

red toward the rear fork arm; the poly-ellipsoidal front headlights positioned along a vertical axle, to contain the front section of the machine, to the advantage of the penetration coefficient. And here, to indicate the dual purpose of the motorbike, I inserted turn lights in the side mirrors, easily removable, when moving from road to track."

Ducati assert that, with the 999, it is feasible to bring the high-performance machine back to the ordinary rider, and then to hand it over to the Superbike competition specialists. A unique fact: Grand Prix motorbikes will never be road bikes and they will always be seen as derivative, like the "Enzo" of the Ferrari F1.

"Everyone has a car," comments Livio Lodi, "and in most cases, this does away with the need for separate or multiple transport. The motorbike today is considered a luxury toy. In the case of Ducati, the rider enters in to a playful symbiosis with the longed-for object. So there is no hesitation in traveling to the office astride one's Multistrada (30% of production is sold to first-time motorcycle buyers), experien-

cing the intoxication of riding a 999 during the lunch break, or riding a splendid Sportclassic to go out to dinner, in delightful company, especially on a warm summer's evening. Of course, one can have more than one car. A motorbike is a choice of incomparable fascination and not to be renounced. With the 2003 Sportclassic, Terblanche reinvented those models that with time have brought prestige to the brand name enhancing their unmistakable importance. The only possible comparison is that of the Mini BMW, which is not a clone of the original Mini Minor design, but a re-working of the essential configuration."

In 1957 Leonard Lord, head of the British Motor Corporation, handed over the job of designing a car of minimal dimensions and maximum comfort to Alec Issigonis. To meet these requirements he restricted the mechanical area to no more than 20% of the available space and reserved 80% to the interior space out of a total length of 3 meters. He laid out the engine transversally with the gearbox underneath, allowing only half a meter for the size

| Sport 1000

of the hood. He then opted for front-wheel drive and excluded the encumbrance of the tunnel over the transmission shaft. He positioned the 10-inch wheels at the four extreme corners of the bodywork. He even managed to include within the allotted interior space, a little trunk with its little external door. Looking at the Mini for the first time in 1959 at the Salon de Paris, Pinin Farina exclaimed: "I can't think of anything to add to it—it's perfect." "A masterpiece," wrote Gianluca Marziani in *Dalla Mini al mini*, "which created a contagious fetishism for the urban passenger compartment. The car was loved for its metallic sensuality, it welcomed the body into a little area of accessible modernity. The Mini was like a garment, or rather a projection of the 'made-to-measure' body, to present itself in the passionate/breathtaking whirl of innovation. Almost 6 million (5,387,862) of Issigonis's masterpiece were sold. And as the last historic Mini emerges from the factory to enter the museum, a new Mini arouses public interest worldwide. This is the version designed by Frank Stephenson. Here, too, the car is not bound by the concept of basic mobility. At a time when cars make their mark with conceptual surplus value set behind an esthetic appearance, the Mini confirmed its unique, overwhelming, inimitable quality. Supremely Mini."

Terblanche concludes: "Here is a sense of the Sportclassic: Paul Smart 1000, Sport 1000, GT 1000, the harvest of an exciting re-reading of the benchmarks in Ducati's history, already described, however, chronologically in this volume with pertinent consideration. The Sportclassic motorcycles incarnate the beauty, timeless style, and the sporting essence of Ducati in the seventies. These are not replicas of period motorbikes, they are today's sports models, or rather custom sports models, not cruisers like the Americans would have designed them. Sportclassic is a project to return to the original unspoilt design at its most expressive, which are and will always remain Ducati. The mobile object is not a painting or a sculpture, it is the fruit of a technological process continually moving forward; the designer is called in to interpret its unstoppable progress. I like to think that today nothing is impossible when a decision is needed about an opportunity to achieve the possible."

Bibliography

Atlante Storico, Garzanti, Milan 1994

Barthes Roland, *Mythologies*, Hill and Wang, New York 1972

Battisti Lucio, Mogol, *Acqua Azzurra*, Edizioni Musicali, Rome 1998

Baudrillard Jean, *The System of Objects*, translated by James Benedict, Verso, London-New York 1996

Bellomo Donatello, *L'uomo che cavalcava un sogno*, Sperling Paperback, Milan 1999

Berti Dino, "La Zirudèla, tiritera popolare," quoted in *Storia della Ducati*, Editografica, Bologna 1991

Bianchi Luigi, Masetti Marco, "Motociclismo racconta la storia della Ducati," in *Motociclismo*, Edisport Editoriale s.p.a. - Motociclismo, Milan 1997

Boneschi Marta, *Poveri ma belli*, Mondadori, Milan 1995

Branzi Andrea, *Introduzione al design italiano*, Baldini & Castoldi, Milan 1999

Carmagnola Fulvio, "Nudi o vestiti?," in *Modo*, no. 154, January-February 1994

Carugati Decio, "Nuccio Bertone e Pinin Farina designer imprenditori," in *Abitare*, no. 398, September 2000

Cavalieri Ducati Bruno, *Storia della Ducati*, Editografica, Bologna 1991

Cherubini Lorenzo (Jovanotti), "La Musica della razza urbana," in *Potere alla Parola*, edited by Pier Francesco Pacoda, Feltrinelli, Milan 1996

Cherubuni Lorenzo (Jovanotti), Cerzosimo Luca, Cecchetto Claudio, *La mia moto*, Edizioni Sony Music Publishing, Dijey's Gang Soleluna, Milan 1989

Colombi Guidotti Mario, *Il grammofono*, Garzanti, Milan 1964

Dalla Lucio, in *Annuario Ducati*, Ed. Ducati, Bologna 1999

Enciclopedia della filosofia, Garzanti, Milan 1998

Enciclopedia della letteratura, Garzanti, Milan 1997

Galli Della Loggia Ernesto, *L'Italia contemporanea 1945/1975*, Einaudi, Turin 1976

Grimal Pierre, *Enciclopedia dei miti*, Garzanti, Milan 1994

Guevara Che Ernesto, Granado Alberto, *The Motorcycle Diaries: A Latin-American Journey*, translated by Ann Wright, Verso, London-New York 1995

Holbrook Pierson Melissa, *The Perfect Vehicle*, Granta Books, London 1997

Loria Aldo, "Note di Viaggio a New York," in *Storia della Ducati*, Editografica, Bologna 1991

Lupi Michele, *Racers*, Feltrinelli, Milan 2003

Marziani Gianluca, *Dalla Mini al mini*, BMW Italia, Milan 2001

Masetti Marco, texts by, *Ducati, una Moto un Mito un Museo*, Editore Le Lettere, Florence 1999

Mereghetti Paolo, *Dizionario dei film 1998*, Baldini & Castoldi, Milan 1997

Monteguti Massimo, *La Ducati*, graduation dissertation, Facoltà di Economia aziendale, Università di Bologna, academic year 1998–1999

"Motociclismo," no. 27, October 1946; no. 31, October 1946; no. 35, December 1946; no. 37, December 1946; no. 9 September 2004 (*Novant'anni di "Motociclismo." La passione infinita*)

Olivero, Maestro, "Ti porterò sul Cucciolo," in *Storia della Ducati*, Editografica, Bologna 1991

Piovene Guido, *Viaggio in Italia*, Mondadori, Milan 1966

Pirsig Robert M., *Zen and the Art of Motorcycle Maintenance*, Vintage Books, London 1999

Pivano Fernanda, *America*, Edizioni Il Formichiere, Milan 1977

Prato Paolo, Trivero Gianluca, *Viaggio e modernità. L'immaginario del mezzo di trasporto tra '800 e '900*, Shakespeare & Company Editore, Milan 1989

Raimondi Giuseppe, "Emilia," in *Cara Italia*, Mondadori, Milan 1963

Thompson Hunter S., *Hell's Angels*, Vintage Books, New York 1998

Venè Gian Franco, *Vola Colomba*, Mondadori, Milan 1990

This volume was printed for Mondadori Electa S.p.A.
by Martellago Mondadori Printing S.p.A.,
Via Castellana 98, Martellago (Venice) in the year 2005

LADY AGRIPPA's
UNSHUTTABLE
CABOODLEBOX

THIS WAY TO THE
PIG AND WHISTLE →

ACKNOWLEDGEMENT

The authors beg to express their
DEEPLY HUMBLE GRATITUDE
to
The Editor of THE DROOP AND BUMPKEITLE DURGE

The RT. HON. LADY AGRIPPA DEADNETTLE,

for her GRACIOUS PERMISSION to borrow
These EXTREMELY VALUABLE ARTICLES
from the
DEADNETTLE COLLECTION

CHUTNI GALORUM NON JAM
TU MAKU SIC

* THE DEADNETTLE FAMILY MOTTO, LOOSELY TRANSLATED AS 'CHUTNEY BY THE TON, NOT JAM,'
REFERS TO THE SIEGE OF CADAVER CASTLE IN 1379 BC, WHEN THE INHABITANTS
TIPPED CAULDRONS OF BOILING GOOSEBERRY JAM ONTO THE ENEMY BELOW. THE
ENEMY, HOWEVER, MERELY SCOOPED IT UP AND SPREAD IT ON THEIR SANDWICHES,
THEN RENEWED THEIR ATTACKS WITH GREATER VIGOUR. LADY AGRIPPA'S
ANCESTOR, LADY NAUSEA DEADNETTLE, SAVED THE DAY WITH 27 TONS OF
HER SPECIAL SCUM AND STINKWORT CHUTNEY. IN HALF AN HOUR THE
BESIEGERS WERE SO ILL, THEY WERE ROUTED WITHOUT A SHOT BEING FIRED.

FIRST PUBLISHED IN GREAT BRITAIN IN 1984
by PAVILION BOOKS LTD, 196 SHAFTESBURY AVENUE, LONDON WC 2H 8JL
in association with MICHAEL JOSEPH LTD, 44 BEDFORD SQUARE, LONDON WC 1B 3DU

COPYRIGHT © 1984 ROBIN AND JOCELYN WILD

Wild, Robin
Lady Agrippa's Unshuttable Caboodlebox
I. TITLE   II. Wild, Jocelyn
823'. 914 [J] PZ 7

ISBN 0-907516-54-8

PRINTED AND BOUND IN GREAT BRITAIN BY BUTLER AND TANNER LTD, FROME.

CONTENTS

FASHION NOTE

LADY AGRIPPA is pictured throughout wearing the original
DEADNETTLE DRY-EYE PICKLED ONION GOGGLES,
invented in 35 B.C. by her ancestor LORDE CARRION DEDDNETTELLE,
and said to have been moulded from the breastplate of Queen Boadicea.
Described as 'The Pickle Maker's Boon,' for their superb efficiency, these
elegant squirt-proof eye cones in flattering Iron Age grey
have recently taken the Fashion World by storm.
Seeing them here on Lady Agrippa, who can be surprised?

HOME COOKING : IN THE KITCHEN AT DEADNETTLE HALL

LADY AGRIPPA, celebrated World Chutney Expert, is seen here in the act of creating a batch of her special CASTOR OIL AND BARNACLE CHUTNEY. Lady Agrippa is wearing her Chutney Making Outfit complete with antique coal scuttle Helmet, Rotating Wasp Repeller and protective goggles for peeling onions. Unfortunately the goggles have got so steamed up she has not noticed that the barnacles, who do not feel at home in boiling castor oil, have wandered off and hidden themselves about the kitchen. CAN YOU SEE ALL 59 OF THEM?

'THE LITTLE KINGDOM': HONEY FOR BREAKFAST

Somewhere in the grounds of Buckingham Palace, London, lies the tiny kingdom of MELVANIA, ruled by the wise and much loved KING HUGO, with his beautiful QUEEN HILDA, and their children, DORA, FLORA, NORA, and DICK. In his private plane King Hugo pays an early morning visit to the royal apiary.

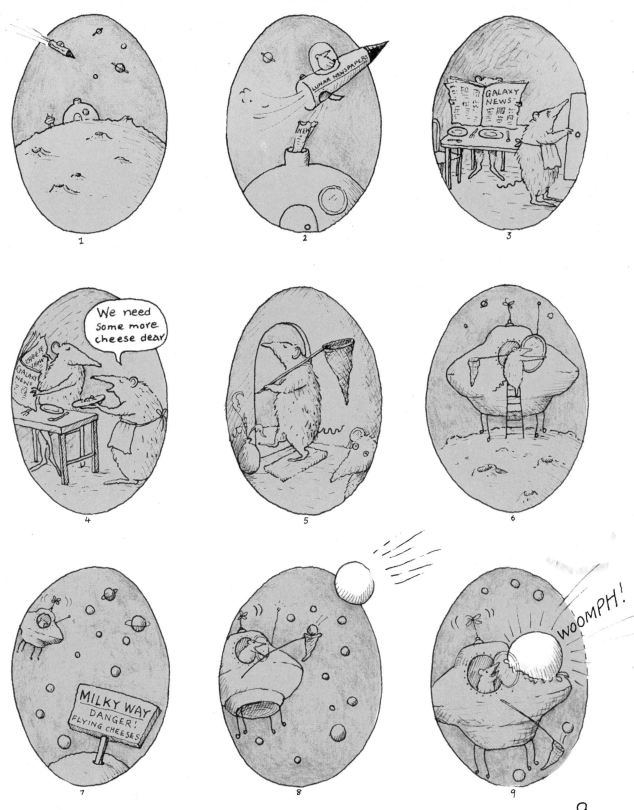

BITS AND BOBS

THIS WEEK'S WETTER

MUDDAY
OOZEDAY
WINDDAY
THAWSDAY
FLOODDAY
SPLATTERDAY
SUNNYDAY

DOCTOR DICK

Poor Doctor Dick is very sick, -
He's caught a bad infection.
And now he's worse,
For here comes Nurse
To give him an injection.

ATTACK!

"Attack, attack!" the General said,
But Private Jones just shook his head.
"If you find battles so exciting
Why don't you do all the fighting? -
I'm going back to bed."

OUR ARTHUR

We bought a little piggywig,
We called him Arthur Tratt,
We fed him milk and barley meal
To make him good and fat.
We patted him and tickled him,
We thought he looked so sweet.
Now Arthur is our little pet, -
He's far too nice to eat.

11

GO FOR A ROW

Hippo gets into the boat. But Anteater gets into the water.

Rescuing Anty is so tiring that Hippo has to have a nap.

A fly comes buzzing round. Anty is afraid it will wake up Hippo.

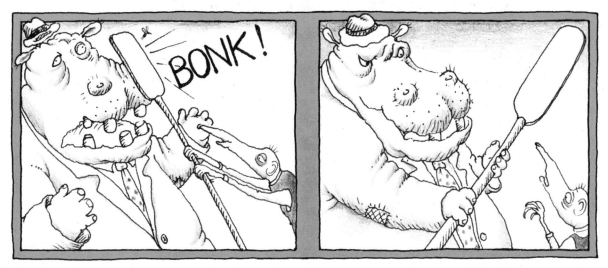

Anteater swats the fly. Now Anteater has woken Hippo.

And Hippo doesn't like being woken up. It makes him mad.

But a refreshing dip in the water soon cools him down.

13

RUNNY HONEY

Winnie won a bunny
And she called the bunny Minnie.
But Minnie was too skinny,
So Winnie said to Benny,
"Benny, Minnie's such a skinny bunny,
Will you ride your pony Tony
To the town to buy a tiny tin of honey?"
Then Benny said to Winnie,
"Winnie, have you any money?"
"Yes," said Winnie,
"Here's one penny."
So Benny on his bony pony Tony
With the penny
Bought the tiny tin of honey
Winnie wanted for her
Skinny bunny Minnie.
But Winnie said,
"You ninny, Benny! —
Can't you see
This honey's
STIFF!
My Minnie likes her honey
RUNNY!"
Then Benny said,
"It's only stiff because it's rainy,

14

Wait until it's sunny, Winnie, —
Honey's only runny
When it's sunny."
When Winnie saw
The rain had gone
She put the honey
In the sun
And soon she saw it
Start to run.
"My brainy Benny's right!"
Cried Winnie,
"Now the honey's nice and runny
I can feed it to my bunny."
As the sunny runny honey
Filled the bunny's skinny tummy
Winnie saw her Minnie start to
Grow and GROW and GROW!
Then Winnie called to brainy Benny,
"Benny, honey,
Come and look, —
My Minnie isn't skinny
Any longer!
She's a bonny bouncing bunny
And she weighs about a
TON!"

Yummy!

GARDENING : THE EDEN OF BUMPKETTLE

IN THE GARDEN AT DEADNETTLE HALL, we find LADY AGRIPPA DEADNETTLE relaxing to the strains of Szqrinchkplopkdin's 79th Concerto for Chainsaw and Pneumatic Drill. Following rumours that a FOX, a RHINOCEROS, an ELEPHANT, a REINDEER, a HIPPO, a TIGER, a SNAKE, a GIRAFFE, a LEOPARD, a BEAR and a LION, missing from Bumpkettle Zoo, have been sighted in the neighbourhood of Deadnettle Hall, Lady Agrippa is wearing the latest in protective headgear, - a Hypnotic Swivelling Eye, ingeniously designed to keep predators at bay.

Lady Agrippa, author of the controversial book 'Pondering the Giant Spinach Weevil', favours the Jungle Look in her delightful garden. Her secret, - a Teaspoonful of her special RATTLESNAKE'S EGG CHUTNEY added to the compost heap.

16

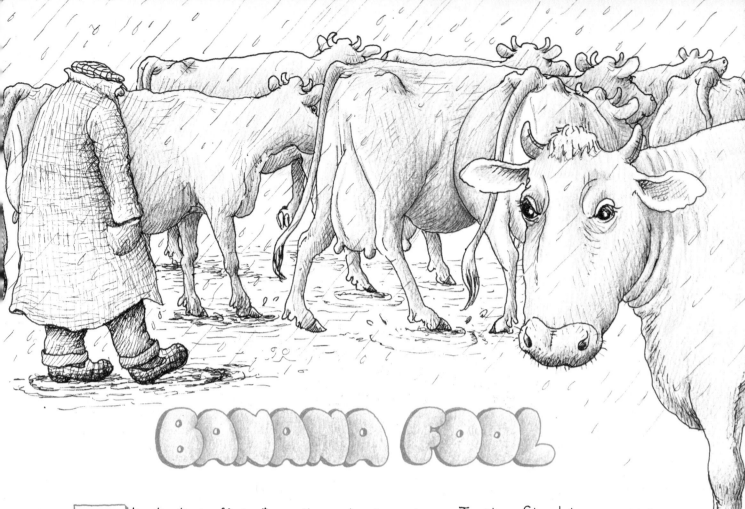

BANANA FOOL

It started off just another boring day. Jupiter Slackheap was driving his cows along the muddy lane, as he did every morning. It was raining, as usual, and Jupiter was soaking wet. His feet were particularly wet, because he was wearing his bedroom slippers. He had forgotten to put on his wellington boots.

A red post van turned into the lane and drove towards him, honking at the cows to get out of the way. It was that nasty Twickenham Pry, the postman, wearing his usual smile of pleasure at the thought of all the bills he was going to deliver.

But today, instead of hurtling past in a spray of mud the red van clattered to a stop beside Jupiter, and a claw-like hand poked out of the window, waving an envelope.

"'Ere, a letter!" came Twickenham's snarl. "Can't be a bill — it's not in a brown envelope." He sounded disappointed. "Says 'PRIVATE.' Let me see now..." he held the envelope up to the light,

"Looks like..."

Jupiter snatched the envelope from the postman's pincer fingers, and as the red van swerved away in a cloud of exhaust fumes he tore it open.

All at once he forgot the miserable pouring rain, the mud, his sodden feet, and the leering postman, as his eyes skimmed over these words...

17

Forgetting all about his cows Jupiter raced back home to tell his wife Gladiola the wonderful news.

When her husband burst into the room with his slippers all covered in mud, Gladiola Slackheap turned off the vacuum cleaner and prepared to turn on one of her screams. But before she could utter a sound Jupiter thrust the voucher under her nose.

"Lovely!" squealed Gladiola, "I'll have a new dress, and a fur coat, and a hairdryer, and an automatic dishwasher, and, let me see... a luxury holiday in the tropics where it's nice and sunny, with palm trees and..."

"Just a minute, they're MY wishes not yours!" snapped her husband, "And I'm going to wish for something nice to eat, as a change from your awful cooking. I wish for my favourite food ~ TONS OF LOVELY RIPE BANANAS!"

His voice was drowned by a tremendous roar. The door crashed open and into the room poured a flood of ripe yellow bananas.

"Help, my best carpet!" shrieked Gladiola. "UGH, they're all squishy!" she screeched, floundering about as bananas buried her up to the waist. "You idiot, - I don't even LIKE bananas!"

"Shut up you old crow!" bellowed her husband, "I'm fed up with your hysterics. I wish a big hairy gorilla would come this minute and carry you off to the jungle!"

Instantly there was a splintering of glass, and a dark hairy arm reached in through the window, seized Gladiola, and dragged her out of the room.

18

Jupiter was rather startled at first, but as his wife's screams faded into the distance he thought how lovely it was to have some peace and quiet at last.

"Well, she said she wanted a tropical holiday," he shrugged, biting into a banana.

But after a little while it began to dawn on Jupiter that from now on there would be no one to cook his dinner, to wash his socks, or to scrub his back in the bath. And the silence, - it was TOO quiet. He would have given anything for just one of Gladiola's bloodcurdling screams. Sadly he tossed away the banana skin and a tear trickled down his cheek.

"She wasn't such a bad old girl really," he sniffed, - "I wish she was here."

And suddenly there was a familiar shriek, and Gladiola came hurtling down the chimney and landed on top of the bananas. But instead of being mad at him, as Jupiter had expected, she screamed out,

"Oh Jupe, it's so good to be home! I never want to go on another tropical holiday. It was nothing but scorpions and mosquitoes. And those horrible gorillas, - UGH! They kept pinching me..." She was interrupted by the telephone ringing. After a frenzied rooting among the bananas Gladiola found the receiver and held it to her ear.

"Hello! . . . Oh dear, are they? I see... yes, I'll tell him." She turned to her husband.

"It's Sergeant Dreadlock at the Police Station. He's asking who your new cowman is. It seems the cows have been reported ten miles up the motorway, heading for Birmingham. Apparently there's a dark thickset gentleman driving them along, - foreign, he thinks, - speaks in grunts, and keeps beating his chest..."

19

"HELP OUR HEDGEHOGS!" CRIES LADY AGRIPPA

Lady AGRIPPA DEADNETTLE, chairman of the Runover Hedgehogs Reinflation Programme, set off today up the Bumpkettle Bypass with her bicycle pump, in a bid to reinflate hedgehogs run over by motorists. LADY AGRIPPA, otherwise known as 'the Hedgehogs' Florence Nightingale', or 'The Lady of the Pump,' denied that hedgehogs purposely linger on roads to puncture motorists' tyres. It was a prickly subject, said Lady Agrippa, speaking between gasps while pumping up a particularly flat specimen. The little creatures are merely trying to make friends with pincushions abandoned by passing motorists. Owing to their habit of looking straight ahead, (hedgehogs cannot look over their shoulder, for obvious reasons), hedgehogs are not able to spot vehicles approaching from behind. Lady Agrippa stressed the importance of hedgehogs in the nation's economy. There were over 30295½ uses for hedgehogs, she declared. The nation's supply of hedgehogs is fast being flattened. They must be pumped up at all costs, and recycled.

BREATHTAKINGLY BEAUTIFUL IN THIS ZEPHYR HELMET AND SENSIBLE HEDGEHOG CAPE, (SYNTHETIC OF COURSE) LADY AGRIPPA DEMONSTRATES HER SKILL AT REINFLATING A FRESHLY FLATTENED HEDGEHOG.

KEEP A HEDGEHOG HANDY

HEDGEHOGS ARE HANDY TO HAVE ABOUT THE HOME. EASY TO STORE, UNLIKE SPERM WHALES OR RHINOCEROSES THE HEDGEHOG FITS NEATLY IN A BOX IN YOUR CORNER CUPBOARD READY FOR ANY EMERGENCY. HARDWEARING AND REQUIRING NOTHING MORE THAN A DAILY SAUCER OF MILK AND PERHAPS THE OCCASIONAL HOLIDAY, YOU'LL FIND HEDGEHOGS FUN TO USE AND AMAZINGLY ECONOMICAL.
RIGHT: ONE OF ITS MANY USES, THE HEDGEHOG CARPET ROLLER, FOR BRUSHING UP THE PILE. CAN BE USED WITH THE DEADNETTLE THRIFT TOOL, (SEE PAGE 64). ALSO USEFUL FOR LAWNS.

ABOVE: THE HEDGEHOG COCKTAIL KIT, FOR PARTIES, SHOWING THE DELUXE MODEL WITH ENCLOSED TRACK, FOR THE HOSTESS WITH NO TIME TO PASS THINGS ROUND.
RIGHT: HEDGEHOGS MAKE EXCELLENT BRUSHES FOR CLEANING DRAINS AND CHIMNEYS. NOTE. DO <u>NOT</u> USE BOILING WATER. IT IS CRUEL.
FAR RIGHT: HEDGEHOG BODY MASSAGER, FOR USE WITH LADY AGRIPPA'S SPECIAL GREASE AND MILDEW CHUTNEY.

ABOVE: THE HEDGEHOG BED OF PRICKLES, FOR MARTYRS AND HOLYMEN.
RIGHT: HEDGEHOG REVOLVING MUDSCRAPER.

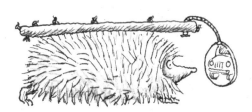

LEFT: IT IS NOT GENERALLY KNOWN THAT HEDGEHOGS SUFFER FROM PRICKLY HEAT. LADY AGRIPPA REVEALED RECENTLY THAT SHE IS WORKING ON A DESIGN FOR A SPECIAL HEDGEHOG SUNBONNET, CONSISTING OF A SLAB OF TOFFEE FITTED WITH A WING MIRROR FOR SPOTTING VEHICLES APPROACHING FROM BEHIND. THE TOFFEE, EXTRA STICKY TO STAY ON THE PRICKLES, ALSO ACTS AS A TRAP FOR FLEAS
BELOW: PICKING GOOSEBERRIES BY PASSING A HEDGEHOG THROUGH THE GOOSEBERRY BUSH.

1

2

← MILK

2

The Moon Mice Set off for Chuckadodo

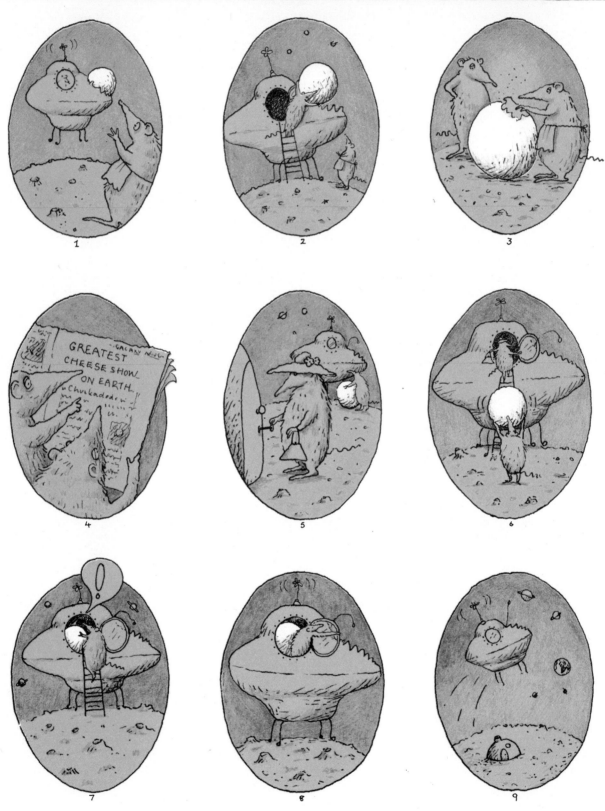

22

THE DROOP AND BUMPKETTLE DURGE

YOUR HYSTERICAL NEWSPAPER

PROFESSOR BOGBEAN SETS OFF

PROFESSOR PODMORE BOGBEAN, the distinguished scientist set off today to the Ubonkme Ibashu Delta, in search of further information to speed the progress of Science. Travelling with only the bare essentials was the key to a successful expedition, said the Professor, famous for his research into the habits of the Prehistoric Sausage Beetle. Even so, the Professor confided to reporters, one always has a curious sinking feeling when starting out on an expedition. The Professor, who has been charged by a herd of rhinoceros beetles, rolled on by a troop of playful porcupines and tossed by a hippopotamus which he boarded in mistake for a ferry boat, attributes his remarkable survival to his experience as a part time bus conductor in Bumpkettle.

LADY AGRIPPA'S
CHAMBER OF LITTLE HORRORS:
1. SCRIBBLING TESS

They say that when Teresa Mould
Was hardly twenty four hours old
Her parents found the tiny tot
Scribbling on her carry cot.
At first the Moulds were filled with pride.
"Our child's a genius!" they cried.
But as Teresa Mould grew older
Her busy fingers grew much bolder.
Soon the window sills, the stairs,
The bath, the sofa and the chairs,
And every single inch of wall
Were covered in her childish scrawl.
Mr. Mould was in despair.

He said, "We need a change of air,"—
We'll take our trying little daughter
To stay at Tooting-on-the-Water."

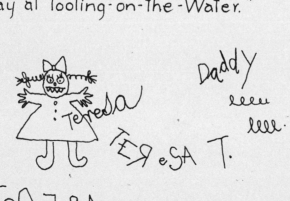

Starting off at nine next day
They passed a castle on the way.
"Let's go inside," said Mr Mould, –
"It looks quite picturesque and old."
Teresa saw a sign in red, –
'Dungeons to the right,' it said.
Unnoticed by the droning guide
She tiptoed from her parents' side,
Along the passage, down the stair,
Through musty chambers dark and bare,
Where spiders hung from chandeliers
Undusted for a hundred years.
"This cupboard's locked!" Teresa cried, –
"I wonder what could be inside?"
She picked a hairpin off the floor
And scratched, 'T. Mould' upon the door.
That instant, with a ghastly din,
The door flew open. From within
A fleshless hand reached out to seize her
And into the cupboard dragged Teresa.
One shriek of terror, sharp and shrill, –
The door slammed shut and all was still.

And now it's quite a famous sight
To see the ghostly child in white
Flitting through the gloomy halls
And scribbling on the castle walls.

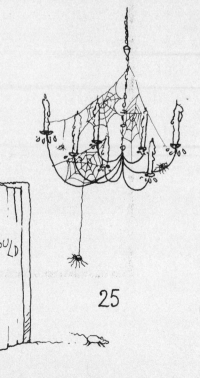

25

'THE LITTLE KINGDOM': KING HUGO'S MORNING RIDE

Out for a ride on his thoroughbred hopper King Hugo meets with terrible dangers. But his quick thinking, and Jumper's bravery bring them both safe home again.

  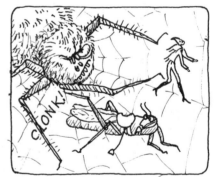

WIN a jar of LADY AGRIPPA'S
SPECIAL SOOT AND TADPOLE CHUTNEY
IN THE DROOP AND BUMPKETTLE DURGE
MYSTERY PHOTO COMPETITION

Just guess what is going on in this remarkable photograph, and send your answer to us by dawn today.
CLUE: THE PHOTOGRAPH WAS TAKEN AT NIGHT.

A flock of four fingered nocturnal jellyfish? To find out turn to page 28

ANSWER to the DROOP AND BUMPKETTLE DURGE

MYSTERY PHOTO COMPETITION!

Well, it's obvious of course: our photo is a charming informal study of LADY AGRIPPA DEADNETTLE, with Bindweed, Sneezewort, Snapdragon, and other members of the famous Deadnettle herd.

Lady Agrippa, who likes to nip out for a drop of hot milk for her bedtime mug of cocoa, has fitted each cow with one of her ingenious Udder Cosies. Skilfully handknitted from luminous caterpillar fur, the cosies not only keep the milk piping hot, but enable the nocturnal milk-maid to find her way to the cow even on the darkest of nights.

President of the Bumpkettle Cattle Breeding Centre, Lady Agrippa is the only known breeder of the unique Deadnettle Boghopper, a breed specially adapted by its unusually flat feet to tramp the quicksands of the Deadnettle Estate without sinking.

Regrettably, Lady Agrippa's own breeding has not equipped her with this feature.

DAWN BREAKS OVER DEADNETTLE HALL

28

THE ANIMAL OUTING

WHICH ANIMALS WENT TO THE SEASIDE?
THERE'S ONE HIDDEN IN EVERY LINE
TO FIND OUT, LOOK ON PAGE 70

Let's all have a picnic at Sandybank Bay, -
A trip to the seaside would be a real treat.
So jump on your bikes, we're off for the day,
We'll have a quick dip and a sandwich to eat.

The water is freezing, - we're all going numb,
I think there's a crab biting one of my toes.
I'm having a go at learning to swim,
But little green fish are tickling my nose.

We're eating our picnic, - the wasps are a pest.
The sun is much hotter, we're all going red.
Millions of ants have got stuck in the jam,
And there's rather a lot of sand in the bread!

Now the sea looks all choppy, it's cloudy again,
Grab your buckets and bathing suits, - here comes the rain!

29

DOCTOR DICK'S ALPHABET

A was Aunt Ada who sat on a snake

B was a Baker who choked on a cake

C was a Crocodile, lame in one leg

D was a Dodo, who laid a bad egg

E was an Elephant, feeling too full

F was a Farmer, chased by a bull

G was a Giant who stubbed his big toe

H was a Hunter, shot by a crow

I was an Insect that fell in some glue

J was a Judge, very ill with the 'flu

K was King Killibog, lost in the wars

L was a Lynx with prickly paws

M was a Monkey who twisted his tail

N was Nurse Nab, blown away in a gale

O was an Ostrich, all tied up in knots

P was a Parson who broke out in spots

Q Queen Quinine, allergic to cheese

R a Rhinoceros, stung by some bees

S was a Sailor about to be sick

T was a Tortoise who swallowed a brick

U Uncle Ug, who got stuck in cement

V was a Viking whose sword was all bent

W was a Walrus who slipped on the ice

X an eXplosion that injured two mice

Y was a Yak who went right round the bend

Z a dead Zebra, and that's the end

HIPPO AND ANTEATER
GO WINDOW CLEANING

Mrs Grimm says yes, she would like her windows cleaned.

Hippo sends Anty up the ladder. But Anty is scared of heights.

Hippo goes up. He is no coward. He tells Anty to hold the ladder.

Hippo sees Mrs Grimm's daughter, and politely raises his hat.

Down falls the bucket of water onto Anty. He lets go of the ladder.

Hippo crashes down, – right onto Mrs Grimm's prize begonias!

THE DROOP AND BUMPKETTLE DURGE
YOUR HYSTERICAL NEWSPAPER

PROFESSOR BOGBEAN LANDS

PROFESSOR BOGBEAN, the famous scientist, was today reported to have made an abrupt landing at Ubonkme Ibashu, after setting out from Bumpkettle Pier over three years ago. The Professor, whose boat, the FLOATING FOSSIL became entangled in a school of Giant Squid, is said to be making a good recovery from his bruises. His unscheduled visit to the North Pole, the breeding ground of the Giant Squid, had afforded a welcome opportunity to get in some practice at knot tying, said the Professor, though if he had known he was going to spend two years on an iceberg with a thousand love sick Giant Squid he would have packed his winter woollies. However, said the Professor, his arrival at Ubonkme Ibashu had proved a most uplifting experience.

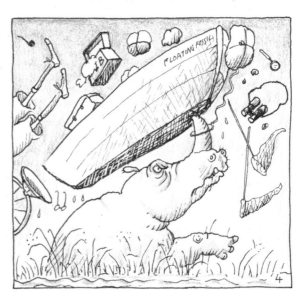

34

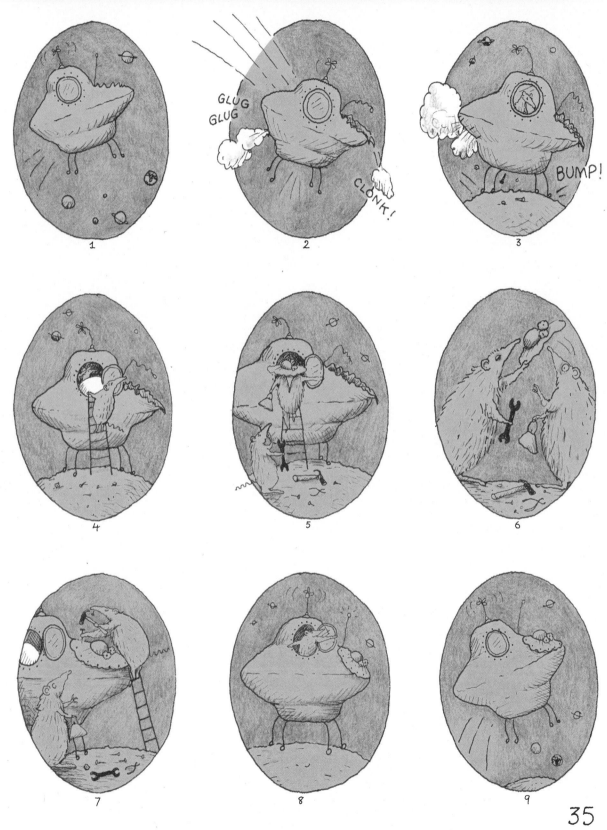

now say these SIX TICKLISH

SHEEP SHEARING

Sasha's shearing Suzy's sheep in sunshine
The sunshine's shining down on Sasha's head
Now Sasha's sick of shearing sheep in sunshine
So she swears she'll shear Sue's sheep in shade instead.

WHATNOT

If gnats could knit and nits could knot
And gnats could sit and nits could squat,
Gnats could sit knitting
And nits could squat knotting
But gnats could not knit squatting
And nits could not knot sitting.

I'm Netty,
the natty
knitter!

I'm the nutty
knitting knotter!

I'm the naughty
knotted knitting
snipper!

EASY WEASEL TEASING

What does a wheezy weasel teaser use to tease a weasel?
Weasel-teasers' weasel teasing tweezers!

36

TONGUE TANGLERS, fast!

FLITTERS

Fleas frisking
Flies flying
Fireflies fire
Flies fall
Fleas freeze
Flies fry
Fleas flee.

JERRY'S JELLY

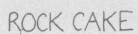

Jerry carries cherry jelly in his jolly jelly lorry.
But if the jelly lorry TIPS
And Jerry's cherry jelly SLIPS, –
Will jolly cherry jelly bury Jerry?

ROCK CAKE

Katy Cockatoo cooked a cake
And took it to Kitty Tit.
"Can't cut it," squeaked Kit.
"Wait a tick, Kit," squawked Kate, –
"Take this Cake Cutting Kit."
So Kit cut Katy's cake
With Kate's Cake Cutting Kit,
And they ate every bit!

37

SEASIDE SCENE

Lady Agrippa Deadnettle, otherwise known as Queen Neptuna of Bumpkettle Bay, has arrived in her single seater Sea Sledge for a seaweed gathering session for her sensational Chutney. While she is snatching a quick snack, see how many different things you can count beginning with S, — in just SIXTY SECONDS!

THE RISE OF RODNEY GLUEBOTTLE

Rodney Gluebottle lived with his Mum at Number 12 Dump View, Seamyside, Bumpkettle. By going out to work every day scrubbing lamp posts Mrs Gluebottle earned just enough to keep them both.

Rodney sat at home all day watching television.

One morning Mrs Gluebottle woke up feeling very poorly.

"Rodney dear," she said to her son, "I'm not feeling too well, so I'm afraid you'll have to go and earn our living now."

Rodney was too engrossed in 'Son of Splatman,' to hear her. All at once Mrs Gluebottle lost her temper.

"GET UP!" she screamed, wrenching the TV plug out of the wall, "AND GO AND LOOK FOR A JOB!"

So Rodney put on his boots and went out to look for work. It was Tuesday, and Mr Pry, the postman, had just collided with a herd of cows, so Rodney got the job of delivering the letters. At the end of the day the Postmaster gave him a stamp for his pay, – a very rare one. But as Rodney was walking home over the bridge the stamp blew out of his hand and fluttered down into the water.

"You crumbwitted prawn!" snapped his mother, when her son returned emptyhanded. "Next time PUT IT IN YOUR POCKET!"

"All right Mum," said Rodney.

Next day, a Wednesday, he got a job in a garden shop, watering the plants. In the evening the manager called him over for his pay.

"Here boy," he said, "take some of this extra strong fertilizer home for your garden."

Remembering his mum's instructions, Rodney crammed as much of the fertilizer as he possibly could into his pockets.

"You plankheaded mango!" screeched his mother, when she smelt him coming up the path. "Next time PUT IT IN A BAG!"

"All right Mum," said Rodney.

On Thursday he worked in a pet shop, weighing out dog biscuits. Seeing how friendly Rodney had become with a little brown puppy, the manager gave it to him as his wages. Rodney remembered what his mum had said, and fetched a paper bag to put it in. But the puppy would not go in the bag. It ripped the paper to shreds and raced away down the street.

39

"You custard-brained tadpole!" screamed his mother. "Next time tie a piece of string to it and PULL IT ALONG!"

"All right Mum," said Rodney.

On Friday he worked in a flooring shop, rolling up carpets. The boss gave him his wages, — a beautiful pale yellow carpet. Rodney carefully tied some string round the carpet and pulled it home. On the way it rained very hard, and when he got home the carpet was no longer pale yellow, but black with mud, and all worn.

When Mrs Gluebottle saw the lovely carpet utterly ruined she gave a moan and fell to the ground. But after a moment she jumped up, took hold of the carpet and hurled it at Rodney with such force it would certainly have knocked him out, if he had not bent down just at that moment to switch on the television.

"Listen, Rodney dear," said Mrs Gluebottle very quietly. Then she suddenly yelled, "NEXT TIME CARRY IT ON YOUR SHOULDER!"

"All right Mum," said Rodney.

Saturday was the weekend, and Rodney, glad of some well earned rest spent the whole day, and Sunday, in front of the television.

On Monday he found work at the Zoo, feeding the animals.

"Here, boy," said the keeper that evening, "You can have this giraffe. It's a spare one."

It was a struggle lifting the giraffe onto his shoulder, but Rodney had promised his mum. Away he tottered down the street.

On his way home he had to pass a block of flats, where the famous pop star, Shrilla Squawkins, lived on the fourth floor. Poor Miss Squawkins had lost her voice after eating a very hot curry. She had accidentally put in a kilo of chillis, when the recipe said a teaspoonful. The doctors all said she would never sing again.

That afternoon Miss Squawkins was sunbathing on her balcony when Rodney staggered along the street below with his load. All at once she looked up, and found herself staring straight into the eyes of the giraffe.

Shrilla opened her mouth, and out came such a shriek that the giraffe took fright, leapt off Rodney's shoulders, and galloped all the way back to the Zoo.

When Rodney trudged up the path emptyhanded as usual his mother was at the door ready to scold him. But just at that moment a huge purple limousine pulled up at the gate. Out jumped a glamorous young lady, who ran up the path and flung her arms around Rodney. It was Shrilla Squawkins. Rodney's giraffe had given her such a fright that the shock had brought back her voice, — louder than ever. She was so grateful she wanted Rodney to join her pop group.

So now Rodney plays the tambourine for Shrilla and the Eardrumbusters, and Mrs Gluebottle makes all the costumes. And I don't have to tell you they are very VERY FAMOUS.

41

2. BUBBLEGUM HERBERT

An ordinary boy was Herbert, –
Fond of lollipops and sherbert
And sticky things which dentists say
Make children's little teeth decay.
But BUBBLEGUM was Herbert's passion,
Gum was what he spent his cash on.
Though Mother begged him not to do it
Herbert simply HAD to chew it.
Now, cows consider it polite
To chew all day, – and half the night,
But people think it's VERY RUDE,
(Except, of course, when eating food.)
And then the BUBBLES Herbert blew, –
A thing no cow would ever do.
His mother shrieked, "No Herbert, stop!"
Next instant there would be a POP!
The bubble burst, and Herbert's mum
Was showered with little bits of gum
Gum stuck to clothes and shoes and hair
Gum was the cross she had to bear.

42

POP!

But now the boy and all his bubbles
Cause his mother no more troubles
For on a breezy summer's day
Herbert simply blew away!
He'd blown a bubble vast and round
That lifted Herbert off the ground,
Above the house and way up high, –
He vanished in a cloudless sky.

Astronomers on watch that night
Observed a most peculiar sight.
It seemed as though a pink balloon
Was floating up towards the moon.
A fortnight later Space Control
Reported: "ROUND PINK UFO
IN SPACE. IDENTIFIED AS HERBERT
JUST SEEN GOING INTO ORBIT"

43

'THE LITTLE KINGDOM': PICNIC BY THE PUDDLESIDE

King Hugo takes the day off from state affairs and treats the Royal Family to a picnic. But while little Prince Dick is playing with his ball he accidentally falls in the water, and the picnic nearly ends in tragedy.

THE DROOP AND BUMPKETTLE DURGE
YOUR HYSTERICAL NEWSPAPER

PROFESSOR BOGBEAN DRIES OUT

PROFESSOR PODMORE BOGBEAN, leader of Bumpkettle's one man Scientific Expedition to the Ubonkme Ibashu Delta, was sighted earlier this week cycling through Hissss Valley, known locally as 'The Snake Pit,' in Central Ubonkme Ibashu. The Professor admitted he was finding it rather hard going, after the theft of both bicycle tyres by a pair of hungry hyenas. However, said the Professor, his experience as a part time postman in Bumpkettle had prepared him for such dangers. Asked if he was aware that only one Traveller in a hundred came out alive from Hissss Valley, owing to the abundance of deadly poisonous snakes in that area, Professor Bogbean said 'what snakes?' He hadn't noticed any.

45

TRANSPORT PROBLEMS FOR LADY AGRIPPA

LADY AGRIPPA DEADNETTLE, leading light of the Bumpkettle Thrift Club, is reported to have set out for Deadnettle Hall after a most successful morning's shopping in the Bumpkettle January Sales. Note her charmingly appropriate head-gear, — a stale Christmas pudding complete with real mould and two dozen realistic imitation pudding weevils.

At the Sales Lady Agrippa has picked up three amazing bargains, — an Expanding GOAT SNAKE, a pedigree BUSH GOAT and a BISCUIT BUSH.

Driving the Deadnettle Bog Sleigh, Lady Agrippa was last seen proceeding at an extremely steady 1 M.P.H. (metre per hour) in the direction of Droop Quicksand, which surrounds Deadnettle Hall. The unique 12 S.P. Bog Sleigh, powered by Giant Irish Bog Slugs, is specially designed for tricky terrain such as Bogs and Quicksands. Unfortunately there is a drawback: it will sink if the driver carries more than one article at a time across the quicksands. Lady Agrippa has a problem. If she takes the snake across, the goat will eat the bush. If she takes the bush the snake will swallow the goat. How can she take all her bargains separately across the bog and get them home safely?

THE ANSWER IS ON PAGE 70.

46

PLADICAPLOTIPUS

I'M A PEDIGREE PLADICAPLOTIPUS,
THE LAST OF THE FAMILY TREE.
I'M A RARE ZOOLOGICAL ODDITY, —
THERE'S NOBODY, NOWHERE LIKE ME,
FOR I'M MADE OF A MIXTURE OF ANIMALS, —
YOU'LL FIND THERE ARE TWELVE IF YOU LOOK,
AND IF GUESSING THEIR NAMES IS TOO DIFFICULT
JUST TURN TO THE END OF THIS BOOK!

MORE BITS AND BOBS

McCLONKEY'S RIDE

1 Billy McClonkey
Hired a donkey
To ride to the Pig and Whistle,
But it started to sway
And its legs all gave way
And McClonkey fell plonk on a thistle.

2 "You can borrow my pony,"
Said Tony Boloney, —
"Just adjust the chin straps and the girth first."
But Bill was adangle
At an odd angle
When both the straps snapped and the girth burst.

3 Some Swedes on an art course
Then lent him their cart horse
Which seemed to be trotting a lot,
Till he saw that the beast
Hadn't moved in the least
But was trotting along on the spot.

4 "Here, have this black yak!"
Said a man from Iraq
"It's under this long matted hair."
Bill whacked the yak's back
But the yak whacked him back, —
Twenty five feet in the air.

5 Said an Arab, "My camel
Is far the best mammal,"
And hoisted him up on its hump.
But it suddenly jumped,
And Billy was dumped,
And the bump came up in a lump.

6 Then a dealer from Delhi
Lent Billy his ele -
Phant, one he had recently fattened.
But it's food had been tainted, -
The elephant fainted,
And Billy McClonkey was flattened.

7 Now the lesson is clear, -
If you feel like a beer
Drink some cocoa instead, or some strong tea.
Shut yourself up inside, -
DON'T go for a ride,
Or you'll end up like Billy McClonkey!

DOWN IN THE GARDEN

Down in the garden where the rhubarb grows
I met an old man with a long red nose.
He ate plum cake with a toasting fork
And stirred his tea with a celery stalk.
"Hello," I called, "It's a lovely day!"
But he snatched up his things and hurried away.

BLACKBERRY PIE

Yummy yum yum, what do I spy?
Here comes Mum with a blackberry pie.
Pour on custard, dig in your spoon,
Gobble gobble gulp, it's gone too soon.

SPIDER

Royston Ryder
Found a spider
Crawling up the bed.
Threw it at his sister
But it missed her, —
It hit the vicar instead.

49

THE LITTLE KINGDOM: PARTY AT THE PALACE

The Head Cook puts the finishing touches to the cake, the maids bring out the jellies and trifles, and lemonade, and everyone is in a happy mood as the guests begin to arrive for little Prince Dick's birthday party.

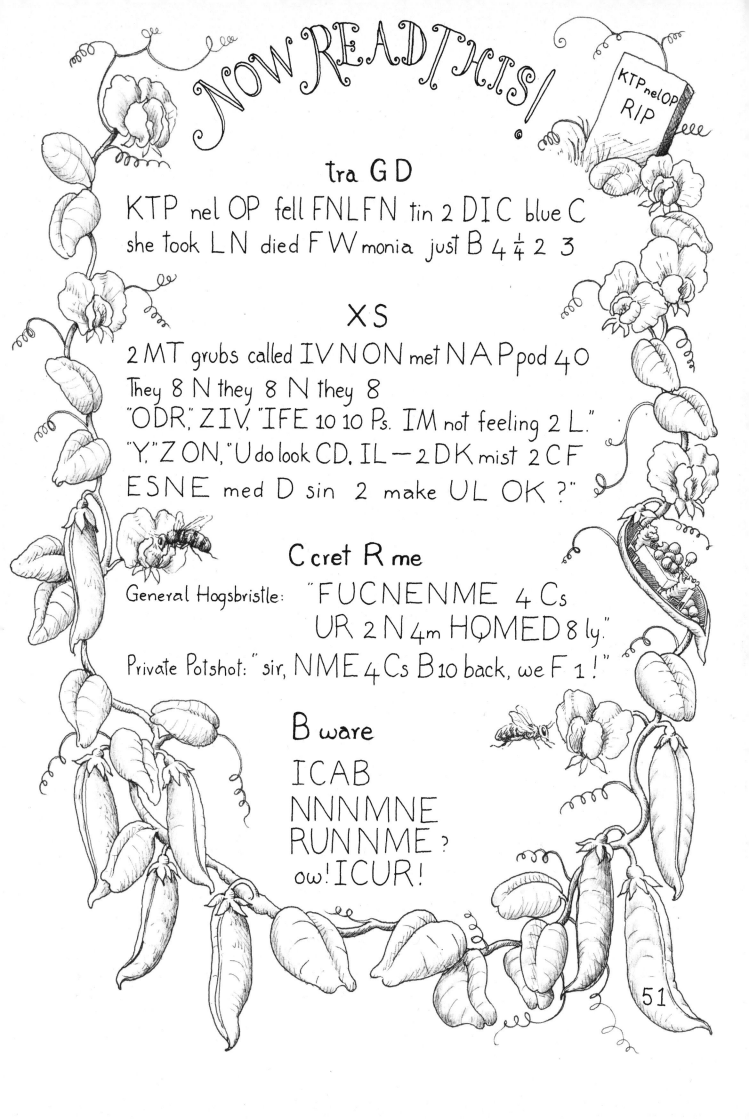

KTP nel OP
RIP

tra G D

KTP nel OP fell FNLFN tin 2 DIC blue C
she took LN died F W monia just B 4¼ 2 3

XS

2 MT grubs called IV N ON met N A P pod 40
They 8 N they 8 N they 8
"ODR," ZIV, "IFE 10 10 Ps. IM not feeling 2 L."
"Y," Z ON, "U do look CD. IL — 2 DK mist 2 CF
ESNE med D sin 2 make UL OK?"

C cret R me

General Hogsbristle: "FUCNENME 4 Cs
UR 2 N 4m HQMED 8 ly."

Private Potshot: "sir, NME 4 Cs B 10 back, we F 1!"

B ware

ICAB
NNNMNE
RUNNME?
ow! ICUR!

FASHION PARADE :-

SPECIAL FEATURE on Bumpkettle's most FAMOUS resident, -

acclaimed in the world of fashion for her ELEGANCE, SUBTLE
FASHION SENSE and UNIQUE STYLE, - LADY AGRIPPA DEADNETTLE.
The following photographs show the SHEER GENIUS with which
Lady Agrippa suits her outfit to the occasion.

Above:
Arriving to judge the
Bumpkettle Bonny Baby Competition,
Lady Agrippa reminds us that
not all rattles are approved by
the Safety Standards Board.
Below: At the start of the
sponsored walk in aid of FHH
(Feed Hungry Hyenas), Lady
Agrippa, wearing this tasteful
gateau in real rubber declares,
"Let them eat cake." Thirty
three competitors started
on the walk, which was routed
across Droop Quicksands.
None returned.

Lady Agrippa at the
Presentation of the
World Cup to China.
This saucy little cup cap
comes with matching
sugar lump earrings
and biscuit freshly picked
from Lady Agrippa's own
biscuit bush.

At the HRS (Hedgehog
Rescue Service) annual
dinner, who could resist
this sensational cactus
bonnet with real sand dune.
Lady Agrippa informs us
that hedgehogs are descended
from a breeding pair of
cacti that escaped when
Sir Walter Raleigh brought
them over from America
together with a sack of
potatoes and a box of
cigars.
Below: Flattering little
outfit for a pressing
invitation to the
Bumpkettle Ironmongers
Annual General Meeting.

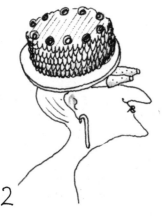

Above: Lady Agrippa
looking 'eggsquisite' in
this 'chic' little hat at
the World Bantamweight
Boxing Championships.
For the Flyweight match
Lady Agrippa's headgear
consisted of a fly paper
bow with single fly
attached.

52

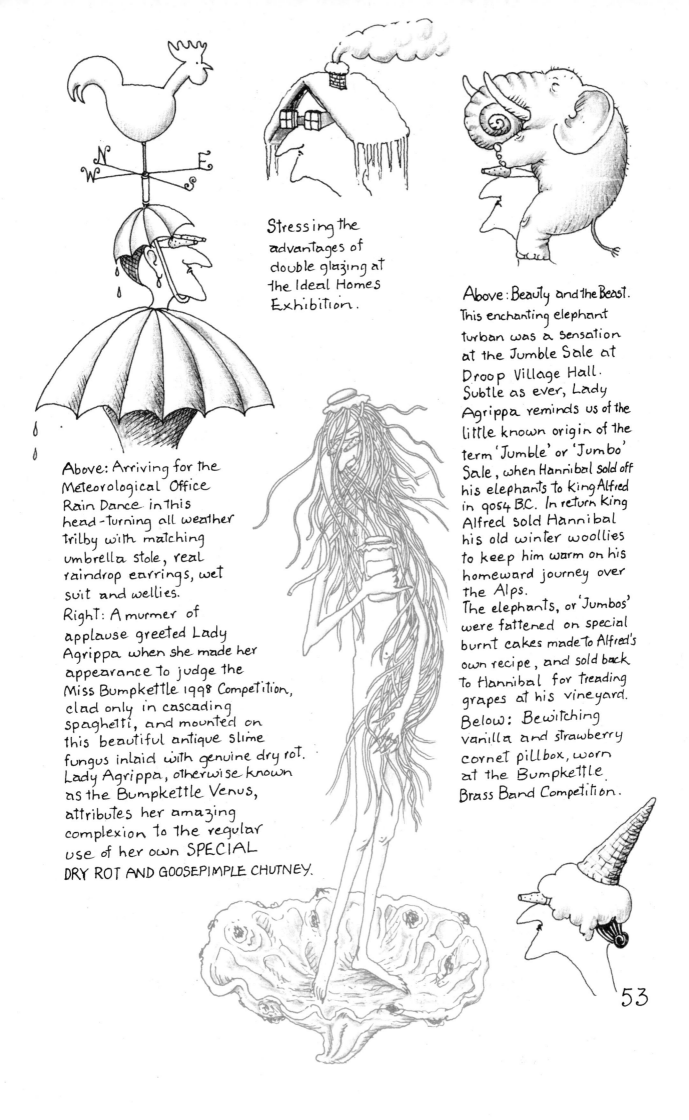

Stressing the advantages of double glazing at the Ideal Homes Exhibition.

Above: Beauty and the Beast. This enchanting elephant turban was a sensation at the Jumble Sale at Droop Village Hall. Subtle as ever, Lady Agrippa reminds us of the little known origin of the term 'Jumble' or 'Jumbo' Sale, when Hannibal sold off his elephants to King Alfred in 9054 B.C. In return King Alfred sold Hannibal his old winter woollies to keep him warm on his homeward journey over the Alps.
The elephants, or 'Jumbos' were fattened on special burnt cakes made to Alfred's own recipe, and sold back to Hannibal for treading grapes at his vineyard.
Below: Bewitching vanilla and strawberry cornet pillbox, worn at the Bumpkettle Brass Band Competition.

Above: Arriving for the Meteorological Office Rain Dance in this head-turning all weather trilby with matching umbrella stole, real raindrop earrings, wet suit and wellies.
Right: A murmer of applause greeted Lady Agrippa when she made her appearance to judge the Miss Bumpkettle 1998 Competition, clad only in cascading spaghetti, and mounted on this beautiful antique slime fungus inlaid with genuine dry rot. Lady Agrippa, otherwise known as the Bumpkettle Venus, attributes her amazing complexion to the regular use of her own SPECIAL DRY ROT AND GOOSEPIMPLE CHUTNEY.

53

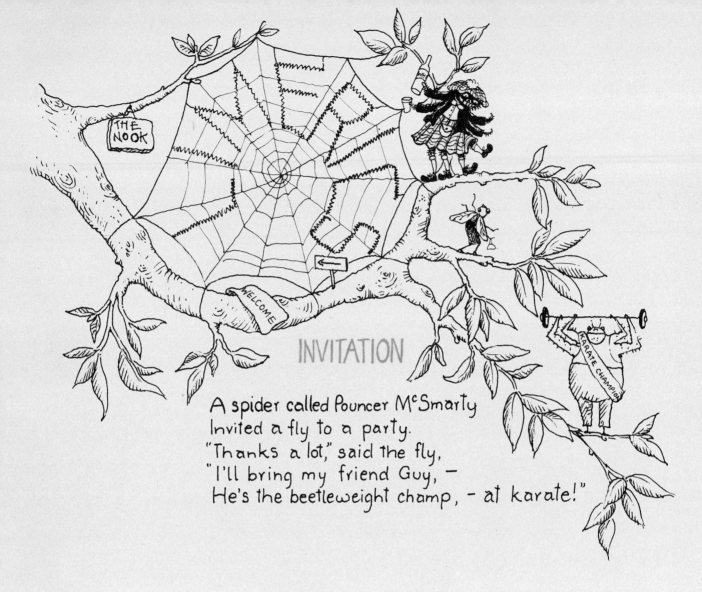

INVITATION

A spider called Pouncer McSmarty
Invited a fly to a party.
"Thanks a lot," said the fly,
"I'll bring my friend Guy, –
He's the beetleweight champ, – at karate!"

DANGEROUS GROUND

There was an old lady who said,
"I really must watch where I tread, –
Just now my bare toes
Felt the cold scaly nose
Of a crocodile under my bed!"

54

WHALES FOR THE WELSH

A well-digger digging in Wales
Always put whales in his wells.
"SAVE THE WHALE!" was his cry,
"If my wells don't run dry
I'll see Wales full of wells full of whales!"

ROLL BLOCK

A gentleman out for a stroll
Was delayed by a stale sausage roll.
He promptly set to,
And chewed his way through, –
Which left the old roll with a hole.

HIPPO AND ANTEATER
GO TO SPAIN

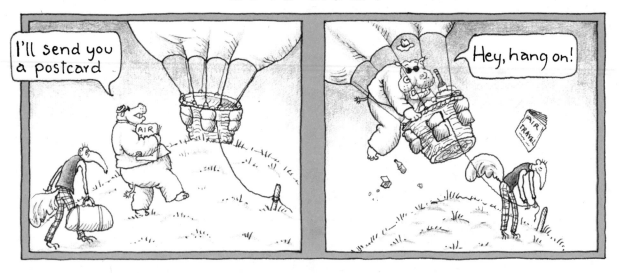

Hippo is off to Spain for a holiday. Anteater unties the balloon.

He forgets to stay behind. It will have to be a holiday for two.

Hippo is in a holiday mood. He celebrates with champagne.

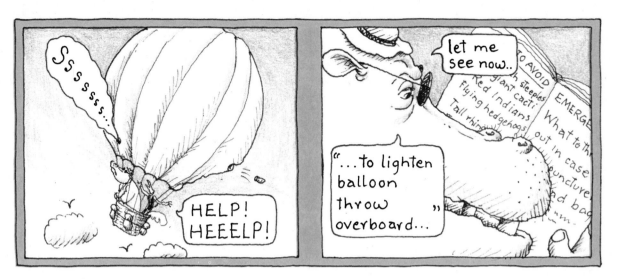

Oh dear! The cork has punctured the balloon. Hippo finds out what to do.

It's all right. Anteater has already dealt with the emergency.

Now there's another emergency. How will he deal with this one?

GHOST

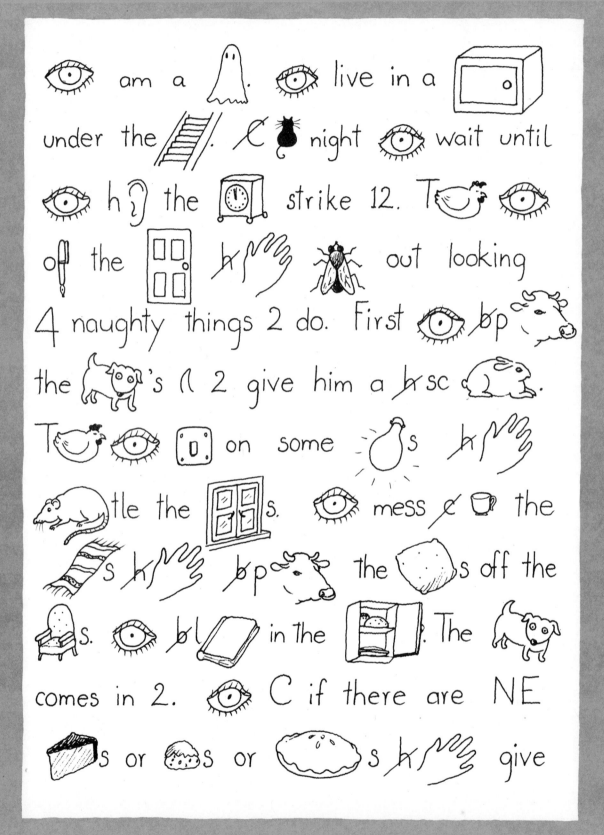

58

STORY

them 2 the [dog]. He eats them b[ball] ¢[cup] b[hand] wags his (l. [eye] do not eat NE myself, 4 B ing a [ghost] [eye] do not k[ill]d NE [foot]t'd.

W[hen] the [sun] rises [eye] must [goat]øt øb[bag] 2 my [microwave] under the [stairs]. MS[moon] [eye] h[ear] the [rocket] of the [house] get out of [bed] b[hand] [goat]øt øt d[clown][stairs]. W[hen] [sheep]øp Cs the mess [sheep]øp is very X. [sheep]øp shouts b[hat] the [dog], he h[owl]s, b[hand][eye] have a [heart]y b[branch][mailbox].

59

3. CATERPILLAR KATE

Mrs Miller's daughter Kate
Scrapes the cabbage off her plate,
And quite unknown to Mrs Miller,
Feeds it to her caterpillar.

Noticing one day at dinner
That her daughter's growing thinner,
Mrs Miller cries, "Why Kate,
Whatever's wrong, – you're losing weight!"

"More cabbage, dear, is what you need.
The doctors say it's guaranteed
To make you strong and help you grow."
(What Katy does with it we know.)

Though cabbages are served each day
The silly girl just fades away.
Now nothing's left of Katy Miller, –
But you should see her caterpillar!

THE LITTLE KINGDOM: AN ENEMY ATTACKS

King Hugo and his subjects are in grave peril when a cat attacks the Palace. The army turns its most powerful cannons on the enemy but in vain. So King Hugo calls out the Wasps of the Royal Air Force.

THE DROOP AND BUMPKETTLE DURGE
YOUR HYSTERICAL NEWSPAPER

PROFESSOR BOGBEAN VANISHES

A rescue party set out today in search of PROFESSOR PODMORE BOGBEAN, the famous scientist and leader of the Bumpkettle Scientific Expedition to Ubonkme Ibashu. Professor Bogbean was last seen collecting specimens of rare stalagmites from a cave on the south face of Mount Mblobu. In a last interview the Professor told reporters that he felt he was on the track of something big. The area, where earlier this year a coach load of tourists suddenly and inexplicably disappeared, is thought to have once been the home of sixty foot long Giant Chameleons, now extinct. The last example of the species was recorded in 1903 B.C.

62

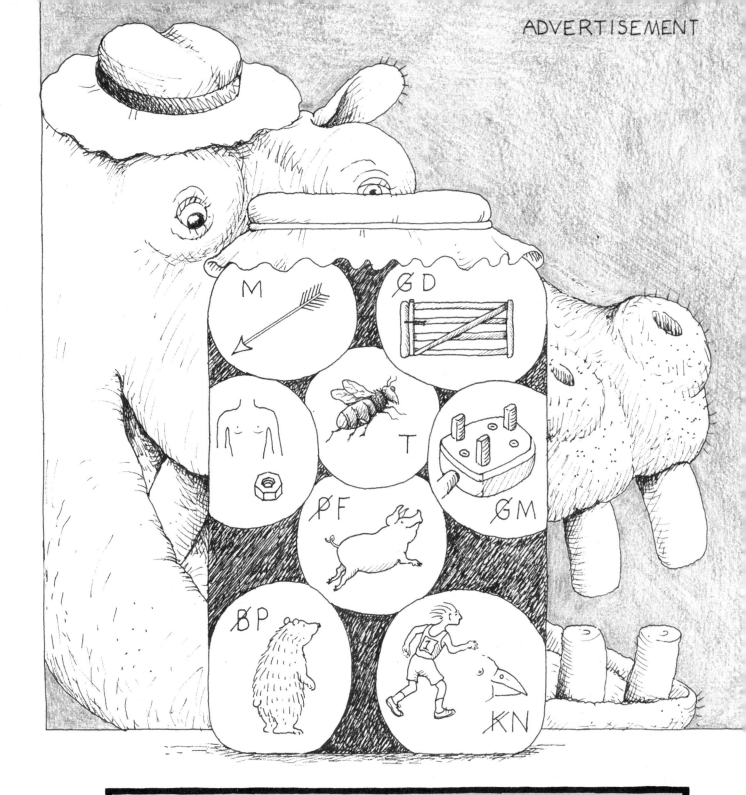

YOU TOO CAN HAVE TEETH LIKE THIS!

For huge yellow teeth like Hippo's, simply treat yourself to
Lady Agrippa's SPECIAL FRUIT AND VEGETABLE CHUTNEY
Just one spoonful will transform your teeth in a twinkling!
It's those eight secret ingredients that will leave you gasping
with surprise! To find out what they are, just turn to page 71.

FOR AN EXTRA HAIRY NOSE LIKE HIPPO'S TRY
Lady Agrippa's SPECIAL HORSEHAIR AND FUNGUS CHUTNEY.
IT REALLY WORKS!

VINEGAR IN HER VEINS

LADY AGRIPPA DEADNETTLE, QUEEN of CHUTNEY

THIS IS YOUR LIFE!

PART ONE :- A GLANCE AT THE DEADNETTLE FAMILY ALBUM

Above, left: Deadnettle Hall, ancient home of the Deadnettles since 1979 BC, when King Alfred gave it to one 'Carrion Deddnettell, grayve digger and pickell mayker,' in payment for 'threee tonne of strong pickelles to eate with ye burnte caykes'. Right: Great great great great great great great uncle Fester Deadnettle, 45th Baronet, who made the historic leap from pickles to chutney, here aged 125, in the Deadnettle Bath Chair, his first and last invention.

Above, left: Baroness Parsimonia Deadnettle, founder of MA (Misers Anonymous) pictured here with the Deadnettle Thrift Tool, a combined pet feeder and carpet sweeper, powered entirely by hungry hamsters. Fondly known as Aunt Ammonia, her influence on the infant Agrippa was profound. Right: the Rt. Hon. Agrippa Ukelalia Deadnettle aged 6 weeks in the arms of her mother, Lady Sloppova, a cement mixer from Vladivostok, with whom Agrippa's father, dashing chutney secret agent 0003X85 QLP fell fatally in love on one of his spying missions to Russia. It was from her mother that Lady Agrippa inherited her unique talent for blending.

64

Left: Agrippa aged 5, as a pickled gherkin at a fancy dress competition at Droop Village Fete.

Right: the teenage Agrippa, in the mountains of Zenophobia, studying the effect on the natives of a diet consisting entirely of her SPECIAL HEMLOCK and TOADSTOOL CHUTNEY (the results were rather striking). Seen with her is a yak in a mac, or 'yaksmac,' the origin of the term 'yashmak,' worn by these animals to keep the rain off their long hair because it takes so long to dry out.
Below: Kyzer Zuke as a kitten

Right: Fiancé Wormwood Blight, the distinguished botanist, receiving the Deadnettle Award for Services to Chutney, seen here with one of his Giant Carnivorous Plants specially bred to halt the march of the Vinegar Fly. Immediately after this picture was taken Mr Blight was reported missing, – a mystery which was never solved.

NEXT WEEK: THE FIRST SOUR NOTE : –
A PLAGUE OF GIANT VINEGAR FLIES...

65

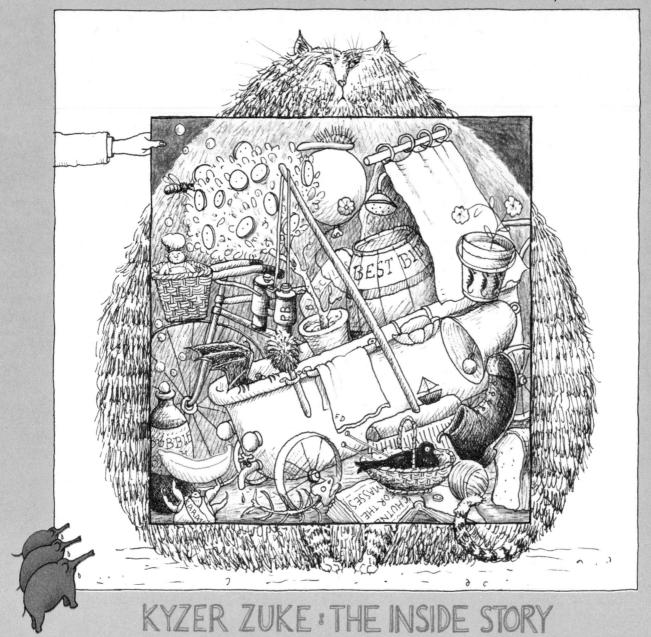

KYZER ZUKE : THE INSIDE STORY

Following reports that a valuable antique Bath Chair was missing from DEADNETTLE HALL, the ancient home of LADY AGRIPPA DEADNETTLE, detectives traced the article to her cat KYZER ZUKE. An Xray on the animal's stomach, carried out by Dr. Dick of Bumpkettle General Hospital, revealed the presence of several items recently reported missing from the locality. The Xray is said to be of great interest to cat food manufacturers, who have observed the curious fact that all the articles begin with the letter B. The National Records Office, which has expressed particular interest in the affair, has confirmed that this represents the greatest number of objects beginning with B to be found in an animal's stomach. (The previous record was held by a Manganese wireback spaniel who accidentally devoured a hundredweight of plastic buttons believing them to be dog biscuits.)

NEWS JUST IN: Three Bedpans and the entire stock of Bandages have just been discovered missing from Bumpkettle General Hospital. Detectives are holding Kyzer Zuke.

MORE NEWS JUST IN: Doctors at Bumpkettle General Hospital are appealing for bandages to bandage detectives scratched while holding Kyzer Zuke.

66

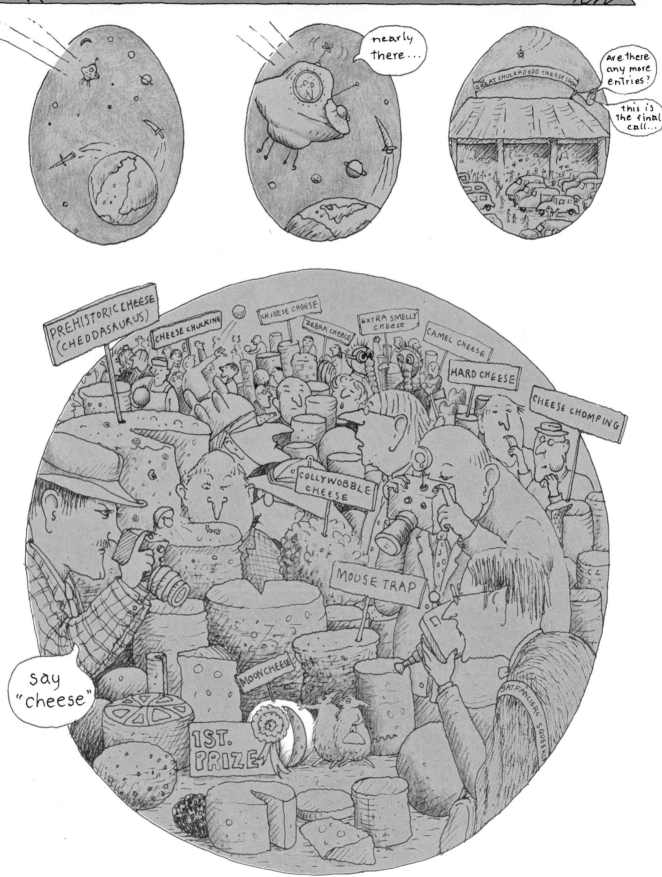

THE WONDERS OF NATURE : SPECIAL REPORT

Field notes reproduced by kind permission of the author, famous scientist and fossil expert PROFESSOR PODMORE BOGBEAN, recently returned from his vitally important expedition to the Ubonkme Ibashu Delta. The Professor, who mysteriously disappeared, made a surprise reappearance from the digestive tract of a 60ft. Giant Chameleon after rescuers poured 306 gallons of Epsom Salts down its throat. The expedition, sponsored by LADY AGRIPPA DEADNETTLE, Editor of the Droop and Bumpkettle Durge, is said by scientific sources to have provided exceptionally valuable information for Science.

Rare Fauna of The Ubonkme Ibashu Delta

Hibernating Nocturnal Tree Slug. The arched back denotes tension due to bad dreams.

Bivalve in attacking position. Bites if handled. When opened this specimen was full of eggs, which were found to be edible, having a pleasant tomato flavour.

North Eastern Himalayan hedgehog and young in moult.

Spider-eating Ground Rat (with prey)

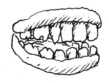

Fossilized jaws of Grranysaurus. On examination were found to contain fossilized traces of prunes and custard.

One-armed Wibble Wobble scratching itself. — A rare sighting as these creatures are extremely shy. Only enemy hungry hyenas.

Spotted Helmet Tortoise (previously thought to be extinct). When disturbed remains motionless for several months. Note camouflage to confuse predators who mistake it for scientist's pith helmet, hence its name.

Remains of Roman Soldier, probably 30,000 B.C., — remarkable condition for age.

P.B.

PROFESSOR BOGBEAN AT HOME

LADY AGRIPPA, an enthusiastic admirer of famous scientist PROFESSOR PODMORE BOGBEAN, has arrived for tea, bearing a jar of her specially matured SEAWEED AND SILAGE CHUTNEY. Eager to hear about his latest expedition to Ubonkmelbashu, Lady Agrippa is particularly anxious to discuss the chutney making possibilities of fossilized Dinosaur Droppings. The Professor, a brilliant scientist, is also a talented home handyman, as can be seen from this view of his delightful sitting room. Lady Agrippa is particularly struck by his Sawn Off Sofa, and matching Sudden Staircase.

ANSWERS

ANIMAL OUTING
29

TRANSPORT PROBLEMS
for LADY AGRIPPA
46

These are the animals that went to the seaside:
CAT BEAR PONY PANDA GNU RABBIT GOAT HARE APE OTTER LION RAT SEAL and BAT

LADY AGRIPPA, otherwise known as the Brain of Bumpkettle, will of course have no problem working out how to get her bargains home without them eating each other. She will take the Goat across first then return for the Snake. Then she will bring back the Goat and leave it by itself while she takes the Biscuit Bush across. She will then return to collect the Goat and proceed with her purchases to Deadnettle Hall, where Kyzer Zuke is awaiting her on the front steps.

PLADICAPLOTIPUS 47

I'VE THE TRUNK OF AN ELEPHANT,
HORNS OF A RHINO,
GIRAFFE'S NECK AND RABBIT'S EARS;
MOUTH OF A CROCODILE,
TORTOISE'S BACK,
AND TWO MORE HORNS, – A DEER'S.
THERE'S A SMALL BIT OF LEOPARD,
SOME STRIPES FROM A ZEBRA,
AND TWO LONG LEGS OF A HORSE;
A BEAR'S FURRY PAWS,
AND LASTLY A TAIL, —
AND THAT'S A PIG'S, OF COURSE!

YOU TOO CAN HAVE TEETH LIKE THIS!

63

Hippo's favourite chutney is one of Lady Agrippa's milder concoctions. The ingredients are listed on the label below.

SPECIAL

FRUIT AND VEG CHUTNEY

INGREDIENTS:

MARROW DATE CHESTNUT BEET PLUM FIG PEAR RUNNER BEAN

71

GOODNIGHT

That's the end, there is no more,
Put out the cat and lock the door.
Kiss goodnight and climb the stairs
Brush your teeth and say your prayers
Between the blankets quickly creep
Close your eyes and GO TO SLEEP.